W9-BNG-107

RX

DEMOCRACY

DEMOCRACY

Edited by Zoe Lowery

Britannica®
Educational Publishing

IN ASSOCIATION WITH

ROSEN
EDUCATIONAL SERVICES

Published in 2015 by Britannica Educational Publishing (a trademark of Ency-clopædia Britannica, Inc.) in association with The Rosen Publishing Group, Inc. 29 East 21st Street, New York, NY 10010

Distributed exclusively by Rosen Publishing.
To see additional Britannica Educational Publishing titles, go to rosenpublishing.com.

First Edition

Britannica Educational Publishing
J.E. Luebering: Director, Core Reference Group
Anthony L. Green: Editor, Compton's by Britannica

Rosen Publishing
Hope Lourie Killcoyne: Executive Editor
Zoe Lowery: Editor
Nelson Sá: Art Director
Michael Moy: Designer
Cindy Reiman: Photography Manager
Amy Feinberg: Photo Researcher
Introduction and supplementary material by Miranda Yaver

Cataloging-in-Publication Data

Democracy/editor Zoe Lowery.
pages cm.—(Political and economic systems)
Includes bibliographical references and index.
ISBN 978-1-62275-356-7 (library bound)
1. Democracy—Juvenile literature. I. Lowery, Zoe.
JC423.D38124 2015
321.8—dc23
2014004688

Manufactured in the United States of America

On the cover, p. 3: *Geri Lavrov/Photographer's Choice/Getty Images*

CONTENTS

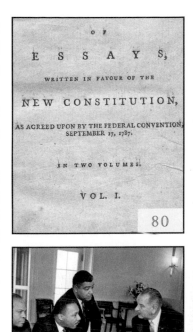

109

133

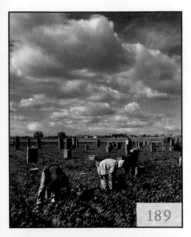

189

190

INTRODUCTION

O ne can scarcely consider analyzing, much less comparing, different political institutions without assessing to
what extent the countries are democratic. This, of course,
begs the question of the qualities that make a country democratic (and to what extent). Is a country simply democratic
or not, or might it be somewhere in between? How do democratic institutions develop in a country? And what are the
implications of these qualities of democracies in terms of
policy and representation?

Theories of democracy have dominated political and
philosophical debates from Classical Greece onward, shaping a number of the foundational texts still read today. From
Aristotle to Tocqueville to contemporary scholars of political science and philosophy, questions of the proper form of
government and preservation of rights have been pursued.
While the Athenian form of democracy entailed more
direct governing by the citizens than we observe in contemporary representative democracy, Aristotle provided early
and foundational claims about deliberative democracy and
the importance of a constitution to organize those inhabit-
ing the Greek city-states, in particular the sovereign office.
It was this constitution that was meant to define the governing body, which in the case of democracy is the people
themselves, as indicated by the word's origin from the root
dēmos, meaning "people." Aristotle noted that in contrast
to an oligarchy where the dominant class tends to be the
wealthy, democracy typically involves rule by the poor—that
is, the masses rather than simply the elite.

The 18th-century philosophic movement laid the foundations for much of what we recognize as democracy today,
with Locke promoting in *Two Treatises of Government* the

Women in Kandahar, Afghanistan, cast their votes for president on Oct. 9, 2004, in the nation's first direct, democratic election. © AP Images

consent of the governed, a claim for which he is often called the father of modern democracy. Here, he additionally put forward a theory of natural law—that which guarantees all men the rights to life, certain liberties, and property—that was later adopted and expanded by Rousseau in France, Kant in Germany, and Jefferson in the United States, among others. It would ultimately be Montesquieu in his *The Spirit of Laws* (1748) who would explicitly advocate the separation and balancing of powers among the executive, legislative, and judicial branches of government to ensure the protection of individual freedoms. Montesquieu held that the executive branch would provide checks on the legislative branch in order to preclude it from "arrogat[ing] to itself whatever authority it pleased" (Book XI), such that this inter-branch relationship would preclude policy from drifting to the extremes relative to the preferences of the people at large.

In his classic examination of American culture and institutions in *Democracy in America*, Tocqueville compared (American) democracy to socialism, holding, "Democracy extends the sphere of individual freedom, socialism restricts it. Democracy attaches all possible value to each man; socialism makes each man a mere agent, a mere number. Democracy and socialism have nothing in common but one word: equality. But notice the difference: while democracy seeks equality in liberty, socialism seeks equality in restraint and servitude." He would spend the lion's share of this famous work exploring why representative democracy has survived in the United States but failed to thrive in a number of other parts of the world.

What has ultimately resulted in the United States is a deep intertwining of democratic government, law, and a culture of rights. Tocqueville declared famously that "[s]carcely any political question arises that is not, sooner or later, transformed into a legal question." That is, he found that a number of America's political questions across history were eventually resolved in the judicial branch. And so American politics and other governments have persisted in developing legal and political principles and laws over recent centuries. The 20th century marked a great expansion in American liberalism as it opened the democratic process to women with the ratification of the Nineteenth Amendment to the United States Constitution in 1920, and amid the civil rights movement and hot contestation over equal protection, the Voting Rights Act of 1965 prohibiting on the basis of race or color individuals' ability to participate in the political process was passed. But while the prohibition of explicitly discriminatory behavior or the expansion of voting rights to broader classes of persons (e.g., those 18 or older) may have a clear association with the fair representation that we associate with democracy, more recent efforts at expanding democratic representation are less straightforward, with no clear answer as to a "fair" redistricting proposal or campaign contribution regulation. And with the growth of the scope of the policies regulated by governments, new questions and complexities arise in assessing the reach of democratic principles.

Democracy can be considered to consist of four core elements: having a system to choose and replace the government by way of free and fair elections; citizens' active participation in politics; the protection of human rights; and the rule of law, which applies equally to all citizens. It contrasts with forms of government in which power is concentrated in a single person, such as in a monarchy. Thus, politics must function based on consent of the governed, with power flowing from the people to their political leaders, who are elected at regular intervals. As the following chapters will demonstrate, democracy can come in multiple different forms, including the parliamentary democracy that one finds in Germany and a number of countries, and the direct democracy system that one finds in Switzerland and at the state level in much of the United States, enabling citizens to themselves put forward legislation onto ballots. Over recent decades and centuries, one can identify numerous revolutions and uprisings with the central goal of defending or promoting the growth of democratic government, a prominent recent example being the United States' occupation of Iraq and subsequent establishment of a democracy therein.

As discussed previously, at the heart of a well-functioning democracy is the protection of citizens' basic human rights and the ability of eligible citizens to have their voice heard through the voting process. It is these "free and fair" elections that often are viewed as bestowing politicians with political legitimacy—that is, the popular acceptance of the leader's political authority to govern. Emphasis on preserving democratic elections has given rise to a growing body of election law that focuses on qualifiers for citizens to vote, reducing barriers to voting, and ensuring equality in people's voices in the political process. Moreover, there must be freedom and pluralism in politics, religion, and the media and governance that is by rule of law rather than by individuals.

With elections worldwide now broadcast from our homes and computers, there is amplified transparency as to the processes by which elections are conducted and to what extent (if any) they are in fact democratic. In the United States, these questions reached perhaps their peak at the time of the presidential election of 2000, which resulted not only in ample ballot confusion, but a division of results between the electoral college and the popular vote, as well as an ultimate resolution in the Supreme Court of the United States, which is comprised of nine politically appointed justices. Subsequent legislation and litigation ensued in the United States in an effort to better streamline state election administration and clarify the appropriate regulations according to which voters should register and be entitled to vote on Election Day.

Federalist structures are those in which the government's sovereignty is constitutionally divided between central and constituent political units (e.g., states or provinces). These types of government structures are based on democratic rule according to which these different institutions govern. Such systems can be found in the United States, Germany, Brazil, Canada, and India, among other countries. The American federal government is comprised of three branches—the executive branch, which is headed by the president, the legislative branch, which includes the House and Senate, and the judicial branch, the most superior part of which is the Supreme Court—as well as having some powers jointly held by state and national governments and some powers reserved for state and local governments. The highly fragmented federal system of the United States—with a vast amount of power bestowed in the state and local governments rather than being centralized at the federal level—has resulted in a system of election administration that is varied from state to state. For example, while some states enable ex-offenders to maintain their rights to vote, others require formal processes to regain that right, and still others permanently revoke voting rights. While some states allow for same-day registration, others require that voters register as much as a month in advance. Further variation can be found with respect to proof of identification at the polls. Thus, the franchise is, though a fundamental right, within certain ranges protected mainly by the lower rather than federal levels of government.

Of course, political participation is not restricted to voting, but rather extends to other forms of political participation—for example, petitioning the government, volunteering, or attending a community meeting—and thus engaging in what is often referred to as "civil society," which comprises organizations that represent a wide range of interests and beliefs in both the public and private spheres. Such groups serve important purposes in furthering political discourse and engagement, better enabling voices to be heard by the elected representatives who are held accountable to the voters in elections.

Yet there are interesting discussions to be had as to the equality of opportunity to participate politically through these means. For example, are the costs of political participation in these informal means the same for working class and wealthy voters? What are the implications if valuable political information is provided in these political venues? Are their interests as well represented in the legislature? The right to participate does not in itself guarantee the right to participate *equally*, a criterion for a well-functioning democracy to satisfy.

An important mechanism for ensuring equal participation, and which will be discussed further in the chapters that follow, is the drawing of district boundaries and the ways in which votes are counted accordingly, with approximately 700,000 voters per congressional district. The 2000 presidential election raised a number of questions as to the merits of the American Electoral College, the institution through which the president and the vice president of the United States are elected by "electors" chosen by popular vote from the states. The winner of the Electoral College—that is, the recipient of 270 or more electoral votes—is declared the winner of the presidency regardless of the popular vote. Critics of this system of presidential election hold that it is inherently undemocratic in nature, bestowing "swing states" (e.g., Ohio, Florida) and other large states (e.g., California, Texas) with disproportionate influence given their winner-take-all systems.

Moreover, while the drawing of district lines is with the goal of ensuring relatively equal numbers of voters per district, their ultimate composition has important implications with respect to minority representation and political competition. While redistricting is a process that is not necessarily politically motivated—and can simply account for population changes—gerrymandering is a much more strategic and self-interested effort at drawing district lines. This brings us to questions about what it means to be represented in politics (American or foreign). On the one hand, we might expect to obtain *substantive representation*; that is, we might demand correspondence between public opinion and the policies that our elected representatives adopt. On the other hand, we might also hope to obtain *descriptive representation*; that is, we might hope to be able to elect representatives who share key characteristics (e.g., gender, race) with large constituencies in the district. To what extent we are ultimately able to achieve either form both depends upon the adherence to democratic principles and helps to further the democratic goals of equality in participation and representation. Moreover, conditions of heightened inequality as well as national security often provide challenging wrinkles with respect to adherence to this democratic representation.

The chapters that follow explore in greater depth the themes discussed previously, tracing the origins and theories of democracy and the factors that enhance and compromise its formation and persistence in the United States as well as in other parts of the world.

CHAPTER 1

DETERMINING DEMOCRACY

Quite literally, the word *democracy* means "rule by the people." Dating back to the Greek *dēmokratiā*, which was coined from *dēmos* ("people") and *kratos* ("rule") in the middle of the 5th century BCE, the origins of the term indicate the political systems then existing in some Greek city-states, particularly Athens.

What Determines Democracy?

Even the very derivation of the term *democracy* suggests there may be more than a few important issues that transcend semantics. If there's any chance of establishing a government of or by the people—a "popular" government—no fewer than five central questions must be confronted at the outset. If the democracy perseveres for long, an additional two questions are sure to present themselves.

1. What is the appropriate unit or association within which a democratic government should be established? A town or city? A country? A business corporation? A university? An international organization? All of these?
2. Given an appropriate association—such as a city— who among its members should enjoy full citizenship?

Situated above the city of Athens, the Parthenon was built in the 5th century BCE *and is considered a symbol of Athenian democracy.* Lambros Kazan/iStock/ Thinkstock

Which persons, in other words, should constitute the *dēmos*? Is every member of the association entitled to participate in governing it? Assuming that children should not be allowed to participate (as most adults would agree), should the *dēmos* include all adults? If it includes only a subset of the adult population, how small can the subset be before the association ceases to be a democracy and becomes something else, such as an aristocracy (government by the best, *aristos*) or an oligarchy (government by the few, *oligos*)?

3. Assuming a proper association and a proper *dēmos*, how are citizens to govern? What political organizations or institutions will they need? Will these institutions differ between different kinds of associations—for example, a small town and a large country?

4. When citizens are divided on an issue, as they often will be, whose views should prevail, and in what circumstances? Should a majority always prevail, or should minorities sometimes be empowered to block or overcome majority rule?

5. If a majority is ordinarily to prevail, what should constitute a proper majority? A majority of all citizens? A majority of voters? Should a proper majority comprise not individual citizens but certain groups or associations of citizens, such as hereditary groups or territorial associations?

6. The preceding questions presuppose an adequate answer to a sixth and even more important question: Why should "the people" rule? Is democracy really better than aristocracy or monarchy? Perhaps, as Plato argues in the *Republic*, the best government would be led by a minority of the most highly qualified persons—an aristocracy of "philosopher-kings." What reasons could be given to show that Plato's view is wrong?

7. No association could maintain a democratic government for very long if a majority of the *dēmos*—or a majority of the government—believed that some other form of government were better. Thus, a minimum condition for the continued existence of a democracy is that a substantial proportion of both the *dēmos* and the leadership believes that popular government is better than any feasible alternative. What conditions, in addition to this one, favour the continued existence of democracy? What conditions are harmful to it? Why have some democracies managed to endure, even through periods of severe crisis, while so many others have collapsed?

Democratic Institutions

The theory and the practice of democracy have both undergone profound changes since the days of ancient Greece, and many alterations have concerned the prevailing answers to questions (1) through (3). Thus, for thousands of years the kind of association in which democracy was practiced, the tribe or the city-state, was small enough to be suitable for some form of democracy by assembly, or "direct democracy." Much later, beginning in the 18th century, as the typical association became the nation-state or country, direct democracy gave way to representative democracy—a transformation so sweeping that, from the perspective of a citizen of ancient Athens, the governments of gigantic associations such as France or the United States might not have appeared democratic at all. This change in turn entailed a new answer to question (3): Representative democracy would require a set of political institutions radically different from those of all earlier democracies.

Another important change has concerned the prevailing answers to question (2). Until fairly recently, most democratic associations limited the right to participate in government to a minority of the adult population—indeed, sometimes to a minuscule minority. Beginning in the 20th century, this right was extended to nearly all adults. Accordingly, a contemporary democrat could reasonably argue that Athens, because it excluded so many adults from the *dēmos*, was not really a democracy—even though the term *democracy* was invented and first applied in Athens.

These and other important changes notwithstanding, a considerable number of early political systems that involved some form of "rule by the people" are easily identified. However, they may not be completely democratic by standards of the present day.

Tribe

A tribe, in anthropology, is a notional form of human social organization based on a set of smaller groups (known as bands), having temporary or permanent political integration, and defined by traditions of common descent, language, culture, and ideology. The term originated in ancient Rome, where the word *tribus* denoted a division within the state. It later came into use as a way to describe the cultures encountered through European exploration. By the mid-19th century, many anthropologists and other scholars were using the term, as well as *band*, *chiefdom*, and *state*, to denote particular stages in unilineal cultural evolution.

Although unilineal cultural evolution is no longer a credible theory, these terms continue to be used as a sort of technical shorthand in college courses, documentaries, and popular reference works. In such contexts, members of a tribe are typically said to share a self-name and a contiguous territory; to work together in such joint endeavours as trade, agriculture, house construction, warfare, and ceremonial activities; and to be composed of a number of smaller local communities such as bands or villages. In addition, they may be aggregated into higher-order clusters, such as nations.

As an anthropological term, the word *tribe* fell out of favour in the latter part of the 20th century. Some anthropologists rejected the term itself, on the grounds that it could not be precisely defined. Others objected to the negative connotations that the word acquired in the colonial context. Scholars of Africa, in particular, felt that it was pejorative as well as inaccurate. Thus, many anthropologists replaced it with the designation *ethnic group*, usually defined as a group of people with a common ancestry and language, a shared cultural and historical tradition, and an identifiable territory. *Ethnic group* is a particularly appropriate term within the discussion of modernizing countries, where one's identity and claims to landownership may depend less on extended kinship ties than on one's natal village or region of origin.

Democracy in Prehistoric Times

Suggesting that democracy was created in one particular place and time—most often identified as Greece about the year 500 BCE—is convenient and tempting. Broadly speaking, however, evidence suggests that even before the 5th century democratic government was practiced in various areas of the world.

It is plausible to assume that democracy in one form or another arises naturally in any well-bounded group, such as a tribe, if the group is sufficiently independent of control by outsiders to permit members to run their own affairs and if a substantial number of members, such as tribal elders, consider themselves about equally qualified to participate in decisions about matters of concern to the group as a whole. This assumption has been supported by studies of nonliterate tribal societies, which suggest that democratic government existed among many tribal groups during the thousands of years when human beings survived by hunting and gathering. To these early humans, democracy, such as it was practiced, might well have seemed the most "natural" political system.

When the lengthy period of hunting and gathering came to an end and humans began to settle in fixed communities, primarily for agriculture and trade, the conditions that favour popular participation in government seem to have become rare. Greater inequalities in wealth and military power between communities, together with a marked increase in the typical community's size and scale, encouraged the spread of hierarchical and authoritarian forms of social organization. As a result, popular governments among settled peoples vanished, to be replaced for thousands of years by governments based on monarchy, despotism, aristocracy, or oligarchy, each of which came to be seen—at least among the dominant members of these societies—as the most natural form of government.

In a few places, conditions became more favorable for the reappearance of democracy around 500 BCE, and a few small groups began to create popular governments. Primitive democracy, one might say, was reinvented in more advanced forms. Two areas of the Mediterranean, Greece and Rome, were home to the most important developments.

CHAPTER 2

DEMOCRATIC BEGINNINGS IN CLASSICAL GREECE

Of course, Greece was not a country in the modern sense during its Classical period (approximately the 5th and 4th centuries BCE). Instead, it was a group of several hundred independent city-states, each with the countryside around it. Guided by the leadership of Cleisthenes, in 507 BCE the citizens of Athens started cultivating a system of popular rule that would last nearly two centuries. To question (1), then, the Greek response was crystal clear: The polis, also known as a city-state, is the political association most appropriate to democratic government.

Polis

Ancient Greece's city-state, or polis (plural, poleis), was a small state in Greece that likely originated from the natural divisions of the country by mountains and the sea and from the original local tribal (ethnic) and cult divisions. There were several hundred poleis, the history and constitutions of most of which are known only sketchily if at all. Thus, most ancient Greek history is recounted in terms of the histories of Athens, Sparta, and a few others.

The polis centred on one town, which was usually walled, but included the surrounding countryside. The town contained a citadel on raised ground (acropolis) and a marketplace (agora). Government was centred in the town, but citizens of the polis lived throughout its territory. Ideally, the polis was a corporation of citizens who all participated in its government, religious cults, defense, and economic welfare and who obeyed its sacred and customary laws. The citizens actually governed in varying degrees, depending upon the form of government (e.g., tyranny, oligarchy, aristocracy, or democracy). Usually the government consisted of an assembly of citizens, a council, and magistrates. Because many poleis had different ranks of

Expansion by Hellenistic kings extended aspects of democracy from Greece to the Middle East. Attalus II Philadelphus, king of Pergamum, founded Antalya, a city on the Mediterranean coast of modern-day Turkey. UIG/Getty Images

citizenship, there were longstanding struggles for political equality with first-class citizens. Each polis also contained substantial numbers of noncitizens (women, minors, resident aliens, and slaves).

In the Hellenistic Age the political freedom of most poleis was curtailed, since they came under the ascendancy of the large territorial monarchies of Macedonian origin. But they continued to manage local affairs, and some, such as Athens, remained flourishing intellectual centres. The Hellenistic kings founded numerous new cities, bringing in Greek and Macedonian settlers who Hellenized part of the local population; in this way the institutions characteristic of the polis spread through much of the Middle East.

Deciding the *Dēmos*

Athenian democracy foreshadowed some later democratic practices, even among peoples who knew little or nothing of the Athenian system. Thus the Athenian answer to question (2)—Who should constitute the *dēmos?*—was similar to the answer developed in many newly democratic countries in the 19th and 20th centuries. Although citizenship in Athens was hereditary, extending to anyone who was born to parents who were themselves Athenian citizens, membership in the *dēmos* was limited to male citizens 18 years of age or older (until 403, when the minimum age was raised to 20).

With data scarce as it is, one must cautiously approximate the size of the Athenian *dēmos*. One scholar has suggested that in the mid-4th century there may have been about 100,000 citizens, 10,000 resident foreigners, or metics, and as many as 150,000 slaves. Among citizens, about 30,000 were males older than age 18. If these numbers are roughly correct, then the *dēmos* comprised 10 to 15 percent of the total population.

Regarding question (3)—What political institutions are necessary for governing?—the Athenians adopted an answer that would appear independently elsewhere. The heart and centre of their government was the Assembly (Ecclesia), which met almost weekly—40 times a year—on the Pnyx, a hill west of the Acropolis. Decisions were taken by vote, and, as in many later assemblies, voting was by a show of hands. As would also be true in many later democratic systems, the votes of a majority of those present and voting prevailed. Although we have no way of knowing how closely the majority in the Assembly represented the much larger number of eligible citizens who did not attend, given the frequency of meetings and the accessibility of the meeting place, it is unlikely that the Assembly could have long persisted in making markedly unpopular decisions.

The powers of the Assembly were broad, but they were by no means unlimited. The agenda of the Assembly was set by the Council of Five Hundred, which, unlike the Assembly, was composed of representatives chosen by lot from each of 139 small territorial entities, known as demes, created by Cleisthenes in 507. The number of representatives from each deme was roughly proportional to its population. The Council's use of representatives (though chosen by lot rather than by election) foreshadowed the election of representatives in later democratic systems.

Another important political institution in Athens was the popular courts (*dikasteria*), described by one scholar as "the most important organ of state, alongside the Assembly," with "unlimited power to control the Assembly, the Council, the magistrates, and political leaders." The popular courts were composed of jurors chosen by lot from a pool of citizens over 30 years of age; the pool itself was chosen annually and also by lot. The institution is a further illustration of the extent to

Metic

In ancient Greece, a metic referred to any of the resident aliens, including freed slaves. Metics were found in most states except Sparta. In Athens, where they were most numerous, they occupied an intermediate position between visiting foreigners and citizens, having both privileges and duties. They were a recognized part of the community and specially protected by law, although subject to restrictions on marriage and property ownership. A significant source of manpower and skilled labour, they constituted a large part of the population of Athens by the 5th century BCE. Cephalus, father of Lysias and a metic, was a character in Plato's *Republic*; Pasion, a metic and former slave, became a great Athenian banker of the 4th century BCE.

which the ordinary citizens of Athens were expected to participate in the political life of the city.

In 411 BCE, exploiting the unrest created by Athens's disastrous and seemingly endless war with Sparta, a group known as the Four Hundred seized control of Athens and established an oligarchy. Less than a year later, the Four Hundred were overthrown and democracy was fully restored. Nine decades later, in 321, Athens was subjugated by its more powerful neighbour to the north, Macedonia, which introduced property qualifications that effectively excluded many ordinary Athenians from the *dēmos*. In 146 BCE what remained of Athenian democracy was extinguished by the conquering Romans.

Ecclesia

The Ecclesia is literally translated as "gathering of those summoned," and in ancient Greece it referred to an assembly

Solon, an Athenian statesman in the 6th century BCE, *ended exclusive aristocratic control of the government and restructured Athens's code of laws.* Carol M. Highsmith/Library of Congress, Washington, D.C. (Digital File Number: LC-DIG-highsm-02101)

of citizens in a city-state. Its roots lay in the Homeric agora, the meeting of the people. The Athenian Ecclesia, for which exists the most detailed record, was already functioning in Draco's day (c. 621 BCE). In the course of Solon's codification of the law (c. 594 BCE), the Ecclesia became coterminous with the body of male citizens 18 years of age or older and had final control over policy, including the right to hear appeals in the *hēliaia* (public court), take part in the election of archons (chief magistrates), and confer special privileges on individuals. In the Athens of the 5th and 4th centuries BCE, the *prytaneis*, a committee of the Boule (council), summoned the Ecclesia both for regular meetings, held four times in each 10th of the year, and for special sessions. Aside from confirmation of magistrates and consideration of ways and means and similar fixed procedures, the agenda was fixed by the *prytaneis*. Because motions had to originate in the Boule, the Ecclesia could not initiate new business. After discussion open to all members, a vote was taken, usually by show of hands, a simple majority determining the result in most cases. Assemblies of this sort existed in most Greek city-states, continuing to function throughout the Hellenistic and Roman periods, though under the Roman Empire their powers gradually atrophied.

Dicastery

A dicastery was known as a judicial body in ancient Athens. Dicasteries were divisions of the *hēliaia* from the time of the democratic reforms of Cleisthenes (c. 508–507 BCE), when the Heliaea was transformed from an appellate court to a court with original jurisdiction. Each year 6,000 volunteers, who were required to be male citizens at least 30 years of age, were assigned by lot to sit on specific dicasteries, or court panels.

Each group of about 500 dicasts (about 200 in matters of private law) constituted a court for the entire year. In more important cases, several dicasteries might be combined. The verdict was determined by majority vote; a tie vote acquitted.

Litigants usually spoke for themselves, though advocates could also speak on behalf of a defendant. Before c. 378 BCE, evidence was presented orally; thereafter, a court clerk read a written brief before the court. Once they had been determined, verdicts were not subject to appeal or revision. The presiding officer of the court supervised only procedural matters; the dicasts were judges of both law and fact and voted on the verdict without discussion among themselves.

The dicastery system has been defended on the grounds that the large number of dicasts provided solidarity against intimidation, lessened the chances of bribery, and made the administration of justice a more democratic process.

Pericles and the School of Hellas

As Athenian leader Pericles gave a funeral address for those who had fallen in the Peloponnesian War in 430 BCE, he portrayed democratic Athens as "the school of Hellas." Among the city's many exemplary qualities, he declared, was its constitution, which "favors the many instead of the few; this is why it is called a democracy." Pericles continued: "If we look to the laws, they afford equal justice to all in their private differences; if to social standing, advancement in public life falls to reputation for capacity, class considerations not being allowed to interfere with merit; nor again does poverty bar the way; if a man is able to serve the state, he is not hindered by obscurity of his condition. The freedom which we enjoy in our government extends also to our ordinary life."

Aristotle's Constitution

The terms of Aristotle's discussion of democracy one century later would have a profound effect on studies comparing political systems. Central to his approach is "an organization of offices, which all the citizens distribute among themselves, according to the power which different classes possess," or a constitution. He concludes that "there must therefore be as many forms of government as there are modes of arranging the offices, according to the superiorities and the differences of the parts of the state." The constant pragmatic, however, Aristotle comments that "the best [government] is often unattainable, and therefore the true legislator and statesman ought to be acquainted, not only with (1) that which is best in the abstract, but also with (2) that which is best relatively to circumstances."

Aristotle identifies three kinds of ideal constitutions, each of which describes a situation in which those who rule pursue the common good, and three corresponding kinds of perverted constitutions, each of which describes a situation in which those who rule pursue narrow and selfish goals. The three kinds of constitutions, both ideal and deviant, are differentiated by the number of persons they allow to rule. Thus "rule by one" is monarchy in its ideal form and tyranny in its deviant form; "rule by the few" is aristocracy in its ideal form and oligarchy in its deviant form; and "rule by the many" is "polity" in its ideal form and democracy in its deviant form.

For more than two millennia, Aristotle's overall structure predominated; however, his indifferent and perplexing definition of democracy—which was probably not shared by most of his contemporaries—did not. Aristotle himself took a more favourable view of democracy in his studies of the variety, stability, and composition of actual democratic governments. All of democracy's advocates in

Deme

In ancient Greece, the *dēmos* was a country district or village, as distinct from a polis, or city-state. *Dēmos* also meant the common people (like the Latin *plebs*). In Cleisthenes' democratic reform at Athens (508/507 BCE), the demes of Attica (the area around Athens) were given status in local and state administration. Males 18 years of age were registered in their local demes, thereby acquiring civic status and rights.

The demes of Attica were local corporations with police powers and their own property, cults, and officials. Members met to decide deme matters and kept property records for purposes of taxation. The *bouletai* (members of the Athenian Boule, or Council of 500) were selected from each deme in proportion to its size. Because the demes were natural districts in origin, their size varied considerably. There were about 150 demes in the 5th century BCE and more than 170 later. A typical deme had three *bouletai*, but the largest had as many as 22.

The term *deme* continued to designate local subdivisions in Hellenistic and Roman times and was applied to circus factions at Constantinople in the 5th and 6th centuries CE.

the years following would strongly emphasize Aristotle's connection between the ideas of democracy and liberty in his observation that "the basis of a democratic state is liberty."

Cleisthenes of Athens

Cleisthenes of Athens was also known as Cleisthenes or Clisthenes (born c. 570 BCE—died c. 508). He was a statesman who was regarded as the founder of Athenian democracy, serving as chief archon (highest magistrate) of the city-state (525–524). Cleisthenes successfully allied himself with the popular Assembly against the nobles (508) and imposed democratic reform. Perhaps his most important

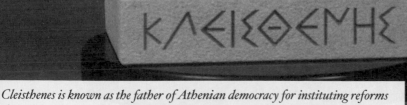

Cleisthenes is known as the father of Athenian democracy for instituting reforms that granted citizenship based on residence in a given township. Photo courtesy of the Ohio Statehouse Photo Archive

innovation was the basing of individual political responsibility on citizenship of a place rather than on membership in a clan.

Cleisthenes persuaded the people to change the basis of political organization from the family, clan, and phratry (kinship group) to the locality. Public rights and duties should henceforward depend on membership of a deme, or township, which kept its own register of citizens and elected its own officials. The citizen would no longer be known only by his father's name but also or alone by the name of his deme. Ten new local tribes were formed to take the place of the four Ionic blood tribes, and, to make faction building more difficult, Attica was divided into three areas—the city itself and its suburbs, the coastal area, and the inland area; and townships from each of the three areas were included in each tribe, ten counties, *trittyes*, being formed in each area for this purpose. And in this grouping steps were probably taken to diminish the local influence of some of the main priestly families. The mixed local tribe became the basis of representation in public office, and the Solonian Council of Four Hundred was increased to 500 (50 from each tribe, with members selected from demes according to their numbers). *Isonomia*, the principle of equality of rights for all, was one of the proudest boasts of the reformers, and there is no doubt that Cleisthenes' work led to a much wider and more active participation by all persons in public life.

CHAPTER 3

ROME'S REPUBLIC

Popular government emerged in the city of Rome as well as on the Italian Peninsula just as it was initiated in Greece. The *rēs pūblica*, or republic, as the Romans referred to it, came from the Latin *rēs*, meaning "thing" or "affair," and *pūblicus* or *pūblica*, meaning "public"—therefore, the thing that belonged to the Roman people, the *populus romanus*, was a republic.

Like Athens, Rome was originally a city-state. Although it expanded rapidly by conquest and annexation far beyond its original borders to encompass all the Mediterranean world and much of western Europe, its government remained, in its basic features, that of a moderately large city-state. Indeed, throughout the republican era (until roughly the end of the first century BCE), Roman assemblies were held in the very small Forum at the centre of the city.

Who constituted the Roman *dēmos?* Although Roman citizenship was conferred by birth, it was also granted by naturalization and by manumission of slaves. As the Roman Republic expanded, it conferred citizenship in varying degrees to many of those within its enlarged boundaries. Because Roman assemblies continued to meet in the Forum, however, most citizens who did not live in or near the city itself were unable to participate and were thus effectively excluded from the *dēmos*. Despite their reputation for practicality and creativity, and notwithstanding many changes in the structure of Roman government over the course of centuries, the Romans never solved this problem. Two millennia later, the solution—electing representatives to a Roman legislature—would seem obvious.

As they adapted to the special features of their society, including its rapidly increasing size, the Romans created a political structure so complex and idiosyncratic that later democratic leaders chose not to emulate it. The Romans used not only an extremely powerful Senate but also four assemblies, each called *comitia* ("assembly") or *concilium* ("council"). The Comitia Curiata was composed of 30 curiae, or local groups, drawn from three ancient *tribus*, or tribes; the Comitia Centuriata consisted of 193 centuries, or military units; the Concilium Plebis was drawn from the ranks of the plebes, or plebeians (common people); and the Comitia Tributa, like the Athenian Assembly, was open to all citizens. In all the assemblies, votes were counted by units (centuries or tribes) rather than by individuals; thus, insofar as a majority prevailed in voting, it would have been a majority of units, not of citizens.

Although they collectively represented all Roman citizens, the assemblies were not sovereign. Throughout the entire period of the republic, the Senate—an institution inherited from the earlier era of the Roman monarchy—continued to exercise great power. Senators were chosen indirectly by the Comitia Centuriata; during the monarchy, they were drawn exclusively from the privileged patrician class, though later, during the republic, members of certain plebeian families were also admitted.

Republic

When representatives of the citizen body rule the state, the form of government is called a republic. The basis on which modern republics are founded is the knowledge that sovereignty lies with the people. However, the category of people—who is included and excluded—has changed through the years. Republics may also stand apart from direct democracy because citizens govern the state by way of representatives; however, modern representative democracies are generally republics.

Prior to the 17th century, the term *republic* was used to designate any state, with the exception of tyrannical regimes. Derived from the Latin expression *rēs pūblica* ("the public thing"), the category of republic could encompass not only democratic states but also oligarchies, aristocracies, and monarchies. In "Six Books of the Commonwealth" (1576), his canonical study of sovereignty, the French political philosopher Jean Bodin thus offers a far-reaching definition of the republic: "the rightly ordered government of a number of families, and of those things which are their common concern, by a sovereign power." Tyrannies were, however, excluded from this definition, since their object is not the common good but the private benefit of one individual.

During the 17th and 18th centuries, the meaning of *republic* shifted with the growing resistance to absolutist regimes and their upheaval in a series of revolutions, from the Eighty Years' War (1568–1648) to the American Revolution (1775–83) and the French Revolution (1787–89). Shaped by those events, the term *republic* came to designate a form of government in which the leader is periodically appointed under a constitution, in contrast to hereditary monarchies.

Despite its democratic implications, the term *republic* was claimed in the 20th century by states whose leadership enjoyed more power than most traditional monarchs, including military dictatorships such as the Republic of Chile under Augusto Pinochet and totalitarian regimes such as the Democratic People's Republic of Korea.

Forum

Forum, in Roman cities in antiquity, referred to a multipurpose, centrally located open area that was surrounded by public buildings and colonnades and that served as a public gathering place. It was an orderly spatial adaptation of the Greek agora, or marketplace, and acropolis.

In the laws of the Twelve Tables the word is used for the vestibule of a tomb; in a Roman camp the forum was an open place beside the praetorium, and the term was originally applied generally to the space in front of any public building or gateway.

The ruins of the Roman Forum, once a bustling gathering place for Roman citizens, remain a popular tourist attraction. Photos.com/Thinkstock

In Rome itself the word *forum* denoted the flat and formerly marshy space between the Palatine and Capitoline hills (also called *forum Romanum*), which even during the regal period accommodated such public meetings as could not be held within the *area Capitolina*. In early times the *forum Romanum* was used for gladiatorial games, and over the colonnades were galleries for spectators; there were also shops of various kinds. Under the Roman Empire, when the forum became primarily a centre for religious and secular spectacles and ceremonies, it was the site of many of the city's most imposing temples and monuments. Among the structures surviving in whole or in part are the Temple of Castor and Pollux, the Temple of the Deified Caesar, the Mamertine Prison, the Curia (Senate house), the Temple of Saturn, the Temple of Vesta, the Temple of Romulus, the Arch of Titus, the Arch of Septimius Severus, and the Cloaca Maxima.

Forum Architect and Engineer: Apollodorus of Damascus

Apollodorus of Damascus was a Damascus-born Greek engineer and architect who worked primarily for the Roman emperor Trajan (reigned 98–117). Apollodorus is credited with the design of most of the imperial buildings erected under Trajan, including the baths, forum, column, and public market that bear Trajan's name, as well as the Ulpian basilica in Rome (also named for the emperor) and the impressive bridge over the Danube (Trajan's Bridge) at what is now Drobeta-Turnu Severin, Romania. Apollodorus is known to have written several technical treatises, though none survive. He was banished by the emperor Hadrian—perhaps following a disagreement about a temple design—and executed about 130.

Also during the imperial period a considerable number of new forums, the *fora civilia* (judicial) and *venalia* (mercantile), came into existence. In addition to the *forum Romanum*, the forums of Caesar and Augustus belonged to the former class, the *forum boarium* (cattle), *holitorium* (vegetable), etc., to the latter.

The 1st-century-BCE architect Vitruvius stated that the ideal forum should be large enough to accommodate a large crowd but not so large as to dwarf a small one. He proposed a 3:2 length-to-breadth ratio. It is to this proportion that Trajan's Forum in Rome was erected early in the 2nd century CE. Commissioned by the emperor Trajan and designed by Apollodorus of Damascus, it measures approximately 920 by 620 feet (about 280 by 190 m) and covers about 25 acres (10 ha). Persons entered through a triple gateway into a colonnaded open space lined with merchants' booths. The forum is flanked by two semicircular, colonnaded exedrae. Opposite the gateway is the Basilica Ulpia, beyond which is Trajan's Column, carved with relief sculpture depicting Trajan's victories. The aesthetic harmony of this space has influenced many subsequent town planners.

The forum was generally paved, and, although on festal occasions chariots were driven through, it was not a thoroughfare and was enclosed by gates at the entrances, of which traces have been found at Pompeii.

Senate

The Senate, in ancient Rome, was the governing and advisory council that proved to be the most permanent element in the Roman constitution. Under the early monarchy the Senate developed as an advisory council; in 509 BCE it contained 300 members, and a distinction existed within it between the heads of the greater and of the lesser families. Throughout the monarchical period the Senate consisted entirely of patricians, and its powers at this time were indefinite.

With the abolition of the monarchy in Rome in 509 BCE, the Senate became the advisory council of the consuls (the two highest magistrates), meeting only at their pleasure and owing its appointment to them; it thus remained a power secondary to the magistrates. However, the consuls held office only for one year, whereas the Senate was a permanent body; in experience and prestige, its individual members were often superior to the consuls of the year. A consul would seldom venture to disregard the advice of the Senate, especially because he himself, in accordance with steadily growing custom, would become a senator at the end of his year of office. (It was probably in their capacity of former magistrates that plebeians first entered the Senate.) But in the early republic the Senate remained an advising body and assumed no definite executive powers.

Consul

In ancient Rome, the consul was either of the two highest of the ordinary magistracies in the ancient Roman Republic. After the fall of the kings (c. 509 BCE) the consulship preserved regal power in a qualified form. Absolute authority was expressed in the consul's imperium (q.v.), but its arbitrary exercise was limited. The consuls, nominated by the Senate and elected by the people in the Comitia Centuriata (a popular assembly), held office for only a year, and each consul had power of veto over the other's decisions. After the establishment of other magistracies, especially the censorship and tribuneship, consular authority was further limited. Consuls, however, were in a very real sense the heads of state. They commanded the army, convened and presided over the Senate and the popular assemblies and executed their decrees, and represented the state in foreign affairs. They retained important prerogatives in administration and in criminal law, and their office was invested with the *sella curulis* (a special chair of office) and an escort of 12 lictors. After 367 BCE at least one of the consuls had to be a plebeian, though in practice the consulship was usually limited to wealthy and noble families with distinguished records of public service. When their terms expired, consuls generally were appointed to serve as governors of provinces. These could be and often were profitable sinecures; in the late years of the republic, provincial governors used their unlimited powers to enrich themselves at every turn. Although the office of consulship remained after the collapse of the republic (27 BCE), it had lost most of its former power. The appointment of consuls passed from the hands of the people to the state; later yet it fell to the emperor to name consuls.

In the last two centuries of the Roman Republic, a great change took place. The Senate became a self-perpetuating, automatically constituted body, independent of the annual magistrates, and a recognized factor in the Roman constitution, with extensive powers. About 312 BCE the selection of senators was transferred from the consuls to the censors, who normally chose former magistrates. In 81 BCE Sulla secured an automatic composition for the Senate by increasing the number of quaestors to 20 and enacting that all former quaestors should pass at once into the Senate.

Quaestor

The quaestor was the lowest ranking regular magistrate in ancient Rome, whose traditional responsibility was the treasury. During the royal period, the kings appointed *quaestores parricidii* (quaestors with judicial powers) to handle cases of murder.

With the advent of the republic in the year 509 BCE, each of the two consuls, who at first were called praetors, appointed a quaestor to be the custodian of the public treasury. After 447 BCE the tribal assembly elected the two quaestors each year. The quaestorship became the first magistracy sought by an ambitious young man. Later in the century it was decreed that plebeians could hold the office, and the number of quaestors was increased to four. Two served as quartermasters to the two consuls when they were in the field, and the other two stayed in Rome to supervise the financial affairs of the treasury.

As Rome proceeded with its conquest of Italy, four more were added and given responsibility for raising taxes and securing recruits from the conquered territories. Each provincial governor had his own quaestor as quartermaster and tax collector. In the provinces the quaestors sometimes performed military functions as well.

In the 2nd century BCE the minimum age for quaestors was 28 years. After their term expired, they usually entered the Senate. After Sulla became dictator in 82 BCE, the minimum age was raised to 30, the quaestors' entrance into the Senate was made automatic, and the number of quaestors was raised to 20. In 45 BCE Julius Caesar increased the number to 40, but the emperor Augustus returned it to 20 and weakened the powers and responsibility of the office. The quaestors' financial responsibilities were eventually assumed by imperial officers. By the 4th century CE the quaestorship was purely honorary and was held usually by men of wealth for social status.

The *quaestor intra Palatium* of the late empire, newly created under the emperor Constantine I, replaced the praetorian prefect in the internal administration. He headed the *consistorium* (the imperial council), drew up laws and answers to petitions, and was responsible for the list of minor staff officers (*laterculum minus*).

The Senate's powers had by this time extended far beyond its ancient prerogatives. The Senate had acquired more effective control through the observance of certain unwritten rules regulating the relation between Senate and magistrates, to whom it formally gave advice. It became the chief governing body in Rome and tendered advice on home and foreign policy, on legislation, and on financial and religious questions. It acquired the right to assign duties to the magistrates, to determine the two provinces to be entrusted to the consuls, to prolong a magistrate's period of office, and to appoint senatorial commissions to help magistrates to organize conquered territory. Its earlier influence upon foreign policy developed into a definite claim to conduct all negotiations with a foreign power, although the formal declaration of war and ratification of treaties were referred to the people. It often acted as arbitrator in disputes among Italian communities, provincials, or client-states.

Censor and Comitia Centuriata

In ancient Rome, the censor was a magistrate whose original functions of registering citizens and their property were greatly expanded to include supervision of senatorial rolls and moral conduct. Censors also assessed property for taxation and contracts, penalized moral offenders by removing their public rights, such as voting and tribe membership, and presided at the lustrum ceremonies of purification at the close of each census. The censorship was instituted in 443 BCE and discontinued in 22 BCE, when the emperors assumed censorial powers.

The censors, who always numbered two, were elected normally at five-year intervals in the Comitia Centuriata (one of the assemblies in which the Roman people voted). Plebeians became eligible in 351 BCE for the originally patrician office. Judgments were passed only with the agreement of both incumbents, and the death or abdication of one resulted in the retirement of the other.

The Comitia Centuriata was an ancient Roman military assembly, instituted c. 450 BCE. It decided on war and peace; passed laws; elected consuls, praetors, and censors; and considered appeals of capital convictions. Unlike the older patrician Comitia Curiata, it included plebeians as well as patricians, assigned to classes and *centuriae* (centuries, or groups of 100) by wealth and the equipment they could provide for military duty. Voting started with the wealthier centuries, whose votes outweighed those of the poorer.

Although individual senators after 218 BCE were debarred from trading, the control of finance was in the Senate's hands. Three circumstances had combined to bring this about. The censors, who were only occasional officials, were entrusted with the leasing of the public revenues; the Senate could order them to redraft contracts. Second, the details of public expenditure were entrusted to the quaestors, young and inexperienced magistrates whom the Senate could guide. Third, the general control exercised by the Senate over provincial affairs implied its direction of the income derived from the provinces. It also claimed the right of granting occupation and decreeing alienation of public lands. Every branch of state finance was therefore in its hands; it controlled revenue and expenditure and supervised the treasury.

This ever-widening influence and power of the Senate was challenged by tribunes from the time of Tiberius Gracchus onward (133 BCE) and, more particularly, by the military leaders, from Marius onward, who pitted their administrative power against the authority of the Senate. Despite the short-lived attempt of Sulla to reinstate the Senate's ascendancy, the republic collapsed under these repeated blows against the authority of the Senate. As a result of the civil war

By increasing the size of the Senate, Julius Caesar aimed to bolster his own support but also succeeded in making the body more representative of the whole Roman citizenry. Richard Gunion/iStock/Thinkstock

between 49 and 45 BCE, the number of senators (which Sulla had earlier raised to 500 or 600) was seriously depleted. Julius Caesar revised the list and increased the Senate to 900, naturally filling it with his own supporters. The composition of the Senate thus underwent a considerable change: few of the senators who had opposed Caesar survived; the new senators included many knights and municipal Italians and even a few provincials from Gaul.

Because Augustus officially "restored the Republic" (27 BCE), it was essential to preserve—at least outwardly—the prestige of the Senate. Although the emperor did not share his basic power with the Senate, he did allow it to cooperate with him in most of the spheres of government. It was left at the head of the ordinary administration of Rome and Italy, together with those provinces that did not require any military force or present special administrative difficulties. It continued to administer the treasury but was soon overshadowed by the emperor, who allowed it to supervise the copper coinage alone. The Senate received judicial functions and for the first time became a court of law, competent to try cases of extortion in the senatorial provinces. The legislative powers of the popular elective assemblies became very gradually extinct, and decrees of the Senate came to take the place of legislative bills adopted by the assemblies in ordinary matters although they did not at first acquire full recognition as laws. Instead, the Senate lost all its control of foreign policy; and, though it was occasionally consulted by the emperor, it was entirely subordinate to him in this department. The emperor could convene and preside over the Senate, his report and other communications taking precedence; his name also headed the list of senators. He could also select new senators virtually at will. Ordinarily, they numbered 300.

The number of Italian and provincial senators increased (especially under Vespasian), but the Italians were not out-numbered by the provincials until after the reign of Sep-timius Severus (CE 193–211). At first the provincials came predominantly from Spain and Narbonese Gaul, but later there were more Asians and Africans. Under Gallienus, senators lost the right to command legions and much of their part in provincial administration. Under Constan-tine they were virtually amalgamated with the knights, who had benefited from these changes. The number of the new senators rose in the 4th century to about 2,000. That the Senate was still regarded as a representative and nec-essary part of the constitution is shown by Constantine's creation of a duplicate Senate in Constantinople.

The most important senators were the great landown-ers throughout the empire, whose position became almost feudal. A great number of them failed to leave their estates to attend meetings, and the Senate often acted—as it had in the early days of the Republic—merely as a town council for Rome, under the chairmanship of the prefect of the city. Many of the great senatorial landowners were men of culture who represented Roman civilization amid increas-ing barbarism and tried to uphold paganism in Italy. In the 5th century, however, some of them helped the barbarian leaders against the imperial authority. In the 6th century the Roman Senate disappears from the historical record; it is last mentioned in CE 580.

Italian Republics (12th to 17th Centuries)

The Italian Peninsula was divided into a jumble of smaller political areas following the 476 collapse of the Roman

Empire. Eventually, some areas in northern Italy would become basically independent city-states and inaugurated systems of government based on broader—but not entirely well liked—involvement and on the election of leaders for limited periods of time. In this manner, these governments could be perceived as small-scale forerunners of later representative systems. In cities such as Venice, Florence, Siena, and Pisa, such governments thrived for at least two centuries.

Not Exactly Democracies

The Italians referred to their city-states as republics, rather than democracies, deciding to call on Latin rather than Greek. Initially, only nobility and large landowners were permitted membership in the *dēmos*; however during the first half of the 13th century in some republic groups from lower social and economic classes—such as the recently rich, smaller merchants and bankers, skilled craftsmen organized in guilds, and foot soldiers commanded by knights—began to demand the right to participate in government at some level. Because they were more numerous than the upper classes and because they threatened (and sometimes carried out) violent uprisings, some of these groups were successful. Even with these additions, however, the *dēmos* in the republics remained only a tiny fraction of the total population, ranging from 12 percent in 14th-century Bologna to 2 percent or less in 15th- and 16th-century Venice, where admission to the ruling nobility had been permanently closed during the 14th century. Thus, whether judged by the standards of Classical Greece or those of Europe and the United States in the 18th century and later, the Italian republics were not democracies.

A more accurate characterization, proposed by the historian Lauro Martines, is "constitutional oligarchies."

In the late 14th century, the conditions that had been so ideal for the presence of self-governing city-states and wider government involvement—especially their economic growth and the civic loyalty of their populations—slowly faded away. Economic decline, corruption, factional disputes, civil wars, and wars with other states led to the weakening of some republican governments and their eventual replacement by authoritarian rulers, whether monarchs, princes, or soldiers.

Quandary in the Democracy

Popular governments were created by the Greeks and the Romans, and the leaders of the Italian republics were pioneers in creating popular governments, with tremendous influence on later political ideas from their commentators and philosophers. Yet the later founders of democratic governments in the nation-states of northern Europe and North America did not emulate their political institutions. As the expansion of Rome had already demonstrated, these institutions were simply not suited to political associations significantly larger than the city-state.

An essential problem comes to light when considering the immense variance in the size of a city-state and a nation-state. By limiting the size of a city-state, citizens can in principle, if not always in practice, directly influence the conduct of their government—for example, by participating in an assembly. But limiting size comes at a cost: important problems—notably defense against larger and more powerful states and the regulation of trade and finance—will remain beyond the capacity of the government to deal with effectively. Alternatively, by increasing the size of the city-state—that is, by enlarging its geographic area and population—citizens can increase the capacity of the government to deal with important problems, but only at the cost of reducing their opportunities to influence the government directly through assemblies or other means.

Many city-states responded to this dilemma by forming alliances or confederations with other city-states and with larger political associations. But the problem would not finally be solved until the development of representative government, which first appeared in northern Europe in the 18th century.

CHAPTER 4

THE THEORY OF DEMOCRACY

It would be almost 2,000 years after Aristotle that John Locke, an English philosopher, wrote his *Second Treatise of Civil Government* (1690), in which he implemented the fundamental components of the Aristotelian organization of constitutions. Locke clearly supported political equality, individual liberty, democracy, and majority rule, unlike Aristotle. Although his work was naturally rather abstract and not particularly programmatic, it provided a powerful philosophical foundation for much later democratic theorizing and political programs.

Locke and Government Validity

Locke championed the idea that in the theoretical "state of nature" that heralds the formation of human civilizations, people live "equal one amongst another without subordination or subjection." He went further to say that they are welcome to act and to do with their possessions however they wish, within the limits of natural law. Using these principles together with others, Locke concludes that political society (i.e., government) to the extent that it is authentic, signifies a social contract among those who have "consented to make one Community or Government . . . wherein the Majority have a right to act and conclude the rest." These two ideas—the consent of the governed and majority rule—became central to all subsequent theories of democracy. For Locke they are inextricably connected: "For if the consent of the majority shall not in reason, be received, as the act of the whole, and conclude every individual; nothing but the consent of every individual can make anything be the act of the whole: But such a consent is next to impossible ever to be had." Thus no government is legitimate unless it enjoys the consent of the governed, and that consent cannot be rendered except through majority rule.

Given these conclusions, it is somewhat surprising that Locke's description of the different forms of government (he calls them "commonwealths") does not explicitly prescribe democracy as the only legitimate system. Writing in England in the 1680s, a generation after the Commonwealth ended with the restoration of the monarchy (1660), Locke was more circumspect than this. Nevertheless, a careful reading of the relevant passages of the *Second Treatise* shows that Locke remains true to his fundamental principle, that the only legitimate form of government is that based on the consent of the governed.

Locke differentiates the various forms of government on the basis of where the people choose to place the power to make laws. His categories are the traditional ones: If the people retain the legislative power for themselves, together with the power to appoint those who execute the laws, then "the Form of the Government is a perfect Democracy." If they put the power "into the hands of a few select Men, and their Heirs or Successors, . . . then it is an Oligarchy: Or else into the hands of one Man, and then it is a Monarchy." Nevertheless, his analysis is far more subversive of nondemocratic forms of government than it appears to be.

Human Rights

Human rights are rights that belong to an individual or group of individuals simply for being human, or as a consequence of inherent human vulnerability, or because they are requisite to the possibility of a just society. Whatever their theoretical justification, human rights refer to a wide continuum of values or capabilities thought to enhance human agency or protect human interests and declared to be universal in character, in some sense equally claimed for all human beings, present and future.

It is a common observation that human beings everywhere require the realization of diverse values or capabilities to ensure their individual and collective well-being. It also is a common observation that this requirement—whether conceived or expressed as a moral or a legal demand—is often painfully frustrated by social as well as natural forces, resulting in exploitation, oppression, persecution, and other forms of deprivation. Deeply rooted in these twin observations are the beginnings of what today are called "human rights" and the national and international legal processes associated with them.

For whatever the form of government, the ultimate source of sovereign power is the people, and all legitimate government must rest on their consent. Therefore, if a government abuses its trust and violates the people's fundamental rights—particularly the right to property—the people are entitled to rebel and replace that government with another to whose laws they can willingly give their consent. And who is to judge whether the government has abused its trust? Again, Locke is unequivocal: The people themselves are to make that judgment. Although he does not use the term, Locke thus unambiguously affirms the right of revolution against a despotic government.

Within one hundred years, Locke's views were echoed in the famous words of the United States Declaration of Independence:

> We hold these truths to be self-evident, that all men are created equal, that they are endowed by their Creator with certain unalienable Rights, that among these are Life, Liberty, and the pursuit of Happiness. That to secure these rights, Governments are instituted among Men, deriving their just powers from the consent of the governed, that whenever any Form of Government becomes destructive of these ends, it is the Right of the People to alter or abolish it, and to institute new government, laying its foundation on such principles and organizing its powers in such form, as to them shall seem most likely to effect their Safety and Happiness.

Fundamental Questions and Answers

For his time Locke had some extreme ideas—they might even be considered quietly groundbreaking. His answers to questions (1) through (3) required additional explanation, as well as some modification, as the democracy's concept and practice of democracy persistently progressed.

Concerning question (1)—What is the appropriate association within which a democratic government should be established?—notwithstanding the generality of his conclusions, Locke clearly intended them to apply to England as a whole, and presumably also to other nation-states. Departing from views that still prevailed among political philosophers of his time, Locke held—as the Levelers did—that democracy did not require a small political unit, such as a city-state, in which all members of the *demos* could participate in government directly. Here again, Locke was at the forefront of the development of democratic ideas.

Regarding question (2)—Who should constitute the *dēmos*?—Locke believed, along with almost everyone else who had expressed an opinion on the issue, that children should not enjoy the full rights of citizenship, though he maintained that parents are morally obliged to respect their children's rights as human beings. With almost no substantive argument, Locke adopted the traditional view that women should be excluded from the *dēmos*, though he insisted that they retain all other fundamental rights. More than a century would pass before "the consent of the people" was generally understood to include the consent of women.

Unlike the men of Athens or the small male aristocracy of Venice, obviously the men of England could not govern directly in an assembly. In this case, then, the answer to question (3)—What political institutions are necessary for governing?—would have to include the use of representatives chosen by the people. Yet, though it seems clear that Locke's government by consent requires representation, he provided little guidance as to the form it might take. This is perhaps because he, like his contemporary readers, assumed that democracy and majority rule would be best implemented in England through parliamentary elections based on an adult-male franchise.

Baron de La Brède et de Montesquieu

Charles-Louis de Secondat, baron de La Brède et de Montesquieu (1689–1755), was a French political philosopher whose major work, *The Spirit of Laws* (1748), was a major contribution to political theory. It inspired France's Declaration of the Rights of Man and the U.S. Constitution.

Montesquieu defined democracy as a republican government in which the people had supreme power and were motivated by public virtue. Roger Viollet/Getty Images

C. DE MONTESQUIEU. 1728

Rejecting Aristotle's classification, Montesquieu distinguishes three ideal types of governments: monarchy, "in which a single person governs by fixed and established laws"; despotism, "in which a single person directs everything by his own will and caprice"; and republican (or popular) government, which may be of two types, depending on whether "the body, or only a part of the people, is possessed of the supreme power," the former being a democracy, the latter an aristocracy.

According to Montesquieu, a necessary condition for the existence of a republican government, whether democratic or aristocratic, is that the people in whom supreme power is lodged possess the quality of "public virtue," meaning that they are motivated by a desire to achieve the public good. Although public virtue may not be necessary in a monarchy and is certainly absent in despotic regimes, it must be present to some degree in aristocratic republics and to a large degree in democratic republics. Sounding a theme that would be loudly echoed in James Madison's *Federalist 10*, Montesquieu asserts that without strong public virtue, a democratic republic is likely to be destroyed by conflict between various "factions," each pursuing its own narrow interests at the expense of the broader public good.

David Hume: Skeptical Philosopher

A Scottish philosopher and historian, David Hume (1711–76) was a founder of the skeptical, or agnostic, school of philosophy. He had a profound influence on European intellectual life. He also strongly emphasized the destructive power of factions and may have more strongly influenced Madison than Montesquieu. For it was from Hume that Madison seems to have acquired a view about factions that turned the issue of the desirability of larger political associations

David Hume believed that small factions threatened a government's stability, an idea that later influenced James Madison. De Agostini Picture Library/ Getty Images

45

(i.e., those larger than the city-state) on its head. For the purpose of diminishing the destructive potential of factionalism, so Hume and Madison argued, bigger is in fact better, because in bigger associations each representative must look after a greater diversity of interests. It is also likely that Madison was influenced by Hume when in *Federalist 10* he rejected the term *democracy* for the type of government based on representation, preferring instead to call it a *republic*.

Jean-Jacques Rousseau: Democracy and Representation

Swiss-born Jean-Jacques Rousseau (1712–78) was a philosopher, writer, and political theorist whose treatises and novels

This statue of Jean-Jacques Rousseau stands in a park in his native Geneva. Rousseau was generally pessimistic about the viability of democracies. Elenarts/iStock/Thinkstock

inspired the leaders of the French Revolution and the Romantic generation. At first glance, Jean-Jacques Rousseau might appear to be a more radical democrat than John Locke, but a closer examination of his work shows that Rousseau's notion of democracy is more limited than Locke's in some crucial respects. Indeed, in his most influential work of political philosophy, *The Social Contract* (1762), Rousseau asserts that democracy is incompatible with representative institutions, a position that renders it all but irrelevant to nation-states. The sovereignty of the people, he argues, can be neither alienated nor represented. "The idea of representatives is modern," he wrote. "In the ancient republics . . . the people never had representatives. . . . [T]he moment a people allows itself to be represented, it is no longer free: it no longer exists." But if representation is incompatible with democracy, and if direct democracy is the only legitimate form of government, then no nation-state of Rousseau's time or any other can have a legitimate government. Furthermore, according to Rousseau, if a political association that is small enough to practice direct democracy, such as a city-state, were to come into existence, it would inevitably be subjugated by larger nation-states and thereby cease to be democratic.

For these and other reasons, Rousseau was pessimistic about the prospects of democracy. "It is against the natural order for the many to govern and the few to be governed," he wrote. "It is unimaginable that the people should remain continually assembled to devote their time to public affairs." Adopting a view common among critics of democracy in his time, Rousseau also held that "there is no government so subject to civil wars and intestine agitations as democratic or popular government." In a much-cited passage, he declares that, "were there a people of gods, their government would be democratic. So perfect a government is not for men."

Despite these negative conclusions, Rousseau hints, in a brief footnote (Book III, Chapter 15), that democratic governments may be viable if joined together in confederations. Some years later, in a discussion of how the people of Poland might govern themselves, he allowed that there is simply no alternative to government by representation. However, he left the problem of the proper size or scale of democratic political associations largely unsolved.

John Stuart Mill and Individual Liberty

John Stuart Mill (1806–73) was an English philosopher, economist, and exponent of utilitarianism. He was prominent as a publicist in the reforming age of the 19th century and remains of lasting interest as a logician and an ethical theorist.

In his work *On Liberty* (1859) Mill argued on utilitarian grounds that individual liberty cannot be legitimately infringed—whether by government, society, or individuals—except in cases where the individual's action would cause harm to others. In a celebrated formulation of this principle, Mill wrote that

> the sole end for which mankind are warranted, individually or collectively, in interfering with the liberty of action of any of their number, is self-protection. . . . The only purpose for which power can be rightfully exercised over any member of a civilised community, against his will, is to prevent harm to others. His own good, either physical or moral, is not a sufficient warrant.

Mill's principle provided a philosophical foundation for some of the basic freedoms essential to a functioning democracy, such as freedom of association, and undermined the legitimacy of paternalistic laws, such as those requiring temperance, which in Mill's view treated adult citizens like children. In the area of what he called the liberty of thought and discussion, another freedom crucial to democracy, Mill argued, also on utilitarian grounds, that legal restrictions on the expression of opinion are never justified. The "collision of adverse opinions," he contended, is a necessary part of any society's search for the truth. In another work, *Considerations on Representative Government* (1861), Mill set forth in a lucid and penetrating manner many of the essential features of the new type of government, which had not yet emerged in Continental Europe and was still incomplete in important respects in the United States. In this work he also advanced a powerful argument on behalf of women's suffrage—a position that virtually all previous political philosophers (all of them male, of course) had ignored or rejected.

CHAPTER 5

TOWARD REPRESENTATIVE DEMOCRACY: EUROPE TO THE 19TH CENTURY

Prior to the 17th century, democratic theorists and political leaders generally turned a blind eye to the very notion that a legislature might comprise neither all citizens, such as in Greece and Rome, nor representatives selected by and from a minuscule oligarchy or hereditary aristocracy, such as in the Italian republics. A crucial fracture in the existing conventionalism came about during and after the English Civil Wars (1642–51) when the Levelers and other radical followers of Puritanism demanded broader representation in Parliament, expanded powers for Parliament's lower house, the House of Commons, and universal manhood suffrage. As with many political innovations, representative government resulted less from philosophical speculation than from a search for practical solutions to a fairly self-evident problem. Nevertheless, the complete assimilation of representation into the theory and practice of democracy was still more than a century away.

Developments in Continental Europe

In assorted areas of northern Continental Europe, freemen and nobles began directly to engage in local assemblies around 800 CE. Later regional and national assemblies were added comprising representatives, many—if not all—of whom were eventually elected. In the mountain valleys of the Alps, such assemblies developed into self-governing cantons, leading eventually to the founding of the Swiss Confederation in the 13th century. By 900, local assemblies of Vikings were meeting in many areas of Scandinavia. Eventually the Vikings realized that to deal with certain larger problems they needed more-inclusive associations, and in Norway, Sweden, and Denmark regional assemblies developed. In 930 Viking descendants in Iceland created the first example of what today would be called a national assembly, legislature, or parliament—the Althing. In later centuries, representative institutions also were established in the emerging nation-states of Norway, Sweden, Denmark, Switzerland, and the Netherlands.

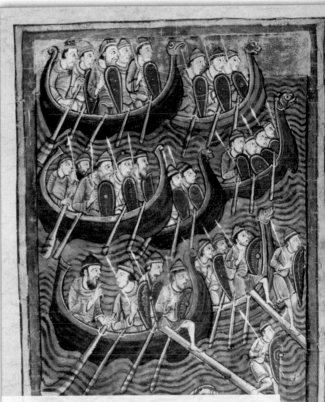

The Vikings, who raided and colonized much of Europe between the 9th and 11th centuries, developed regional assemblies to reduce feuds and maintain social order. Bymuseum, Oslo, Norway/Index/ Bridgeman Art Library

Thing

A *thing*, in medieval Scandinavia, referred to the local, provincial, and, in Iceland, national assemblies of freemen that formed the fundamental unit of government and law. Meeting at fixed intervals, the *things*, in which democratic practices were influenced by male heads of households, legislated at all levels, elected royal nominees, and settled all legal questions. They were presided over by the local chieftain or by a law speaker (one unusually learned in the unrecorded law) and were dominated by the most influential members of the community. In Iceland the *things* ultimately led to the founding of the Althing, the Icelandic parliament. In the 13th and 14th centuries the *things* in other countries gradually lost their prerogatives to bureaucratized courts and noble-clerical councils.

Developments in England

During the Middle Ages, of all the assemblies generated in Europe, the advance of representative government most overwhelmingly changed the English Parliament. Although it was an unintentional result of opportunistic innovations, Parliament developed from king-requested councils in order to remedy complaints and exercise judicial functions. In time, Parliament began to deal with important matters of state, notably the raising of revenues needed to support the policies and decisions of the monarch. As its judicial functions were increasingly delegated to courts, it gradually evolved into a legislative body. By the end of the 15th century, the English system displayed some of the basic features of modern parliamentary government: for example, the enactment of laws now required the passage of bills by both houses of Parliament and the formal approval of the monarch.

Other important features had yet to be established, however. England's political life was dominated by the monarchy for centuries after the Middle Ages. During the English Civil Wars, led on one side by radical Puritans, the monarchy was abolished and a republic—the Commonwealth—was established (1649), though the monarchy was restored in 1660. By about 1800, significant powers, notably including powers related to the appointment and tenure of the prime minister, had shifted to Parliament. This development was strongly influenced by the emergence of political factions in Parliament during the early years of the 18th century. These factions, known as Whigs and Tories, later became full-fledged parties. To king and Parliament alike it became increasingly apparent that laws could not be passed nor taxes raised without the support of a Whig or Tory leader who could muster a majority of votes in the House of Commons. To gain that support, the monarch was forced to select as prime minister the

King George III saw his power as monarch diminished in 1782 when Parliament formed a coalition government of which he did not approve. Photos.com/Thinkstock

leader of the majority party in the Commons and to accept the leader's suggestions for the composition of the cabinet. That the monarch should have to yield to Parliament in this area became manifest during a constitutional crisis in 1782,

Whig and Tory

Whig and *Tory* are terms that refer to members of two opposing political parties or factions in England, particularly during the 18th century. Originally *Whig* and *Tory* were terms of abuse introduced in 1679 during the heated struggle over the bill to exclude James, duke of York (afterward James II), from the succession. *Whig*—whatever its origin in Scottish Gaelic—was a term applied to horse thieves and, later, to Scottish Presbyterians; it connoted nonconformity and rebellion and referred to those who claimed the power of excluding the heir from the throne. *Tory* was an Irish term suggesting a papist outlaw and referred to those who supported the hereditary right of James despite his Roman Catholic faith.

The Glorious Revolution (1688–89) modified the division in principle between the two parties, for it had been a joint achievement. Thereafter most Tories accepted something of the Whig doctrines of limited constitutional monarchy rather than divine-right absolutism. Under Queen Anne, the Tories represented the resistance, mainly by the country gentry, to religious toleration and foreign entanglements. Toryism became identified with Anglicanism and the squirearchy and Whiggism with the aristocratic, landowning families and the financial interests of the wealthy middle classes.

The death of Anne in 1714, the manner in which George I came to the throne as a nominee of the Whigs, and the flight (1715) of the Tory leader Henry St. John, 1st Viscount Bolingbroke, to France, conspired to destroy the Tories' political power.

For nearly 50 years thereafter, aristocratic groups and connections ruled, regarding themselves as Whigs by sentiment and tradition. Die-hard Tories were discredited as Jacobites, seeking to restore the Stuart heirs to the throne, though about 100 country gentlemen, regarding themselves as Tories, remained members of the House of Commons throughout the years of the Whig hegemony. As individuals and at the level of local politics, administration, and influence, such "Tories" remained of considerable importance.

With George III's (1760–1820) reign, the meanings of the two words shifted. No Whig Party as such existed then, only a series of aristocratic groups and family connections operating in Parliament through patronage and influence. Nor was there a Tory Party, only Tory sentiment, tradition, and temperament surviving among certain families and social groups. The so-called King's Friends, from whom George III preferred to draw his ministers (especially under Lord North [afterward 2nd earl of Guilford], 1770–82), came from both traditions and from neither. Real party alignments began to take shape only after 1784, when profound political issues that deeply stirred public opinion were arising, such as the controversy over the American Revolution.

After 1784 William Pitt the Younger became the leader of a new Tory Party, which broadly represented the interests of the country gentry, merchant classes, and official administerial groups. In opposition, a revived Whig Party, led by Charles James Fox, came to represent the interests of religious dissenters, industrialists, and others who sought electoral, parliamentary, and philanthropic reforms.

The French Revolution and the wars against France soon further complicated the parties' division. A large section of the more moderate Whigs deserted Fox and supported Pitt. After 1815 and a period of party confusion, there eventually emerged the conservatism of Sir Robert Peel and Benjamin Disraeli, earl of Beaconsfield, and the liberalism of Lord John Russell and William Ewart Gladstone, with the party labels of Conservative and Liberal assumed by each faction, respectively. Although the label *Tory* has continued to be used to designate the Conservative Party, *Whig* has ceased to have much political meaning.

when King George III (reigned 1760–1820) was compelled, much against his will, to accept a Whig prime minister and cabinet—a situation he regarded, according to one scholar, as "a violation of the Constitution, a defeat for his policy, and a personal humiliation." By 1830 the constitutional principle that the choice of prime minister, and thus the cabinet, reposed with the House of Commons had become firmly entrenched in the (unwritten) British Constitution.

Parliamentary government in Britain was not yet a democratic system, however. Mainly because of property requirements, the franchise was held by only about 5 percent of the British population over 20 years of age. The Reform Act of 1832, which is generally viewed as a historic threshold in the development of parliamentary democracy in Britain, extended the suffrage to about 7 percent of the adult population. It would require further acts of Parliament in 1867, 1884, and 1918 to achieve universal male suffrage and one more law, enacted in 1928, to secure the right to vote for all adult women.

CHAPTER 6

19TH-CENTURY DEVELOPMENTS IN THE UNITED STATES

Thanks to the development of Parliament, representative government was shown to be practicable. Still, it was with the governments of the British colonies of North America and later in the founding of the United States of America that the probability of uniting representation with democracy first became altogether apparent.

Conditions in colonial America favoured the limited development of a system of representation more broadly based than the one in use in Great Britain. These conditions included the vast distance from London, which forced the British government to grant significant autonomy to the colonies; the existence of colonial legislatures in which representatives in at least one house were elected by voters; the expansion of the suffrage, which in some colonies came to include most adult white males; the spread of property ownership, particularly in land; and the strengthening of beliefs in fundamental rights and popular sovereignty, including the belief that the colonists, as British citizens, should not have to pay taxes to a government in which they were not represented ("no taxation without representation").

Until about 1760, most colonists were loyal to the mother country and did not think of themselves as constituting a separate nation of "Americans." After Britain imposed direct taxation on the colonies through the Stamp Act (1765), however, there were public (and sometimes violent) displays of opposition to the new law. In colonial newspapers there was also a sharp increase in the use of the term *Americans* to refer to the colonial population. Other factors that helped to create a distinct American identity were the outbreak of war with Britain in 1775 and the shared hardships and suffering of the people during many years of fighting, the adoption of the Declaration of Independence in 1776, the flight of many loyalists to Canada and England, and the rapid increase in travel and communication between the newly independent states. The colonists' sense of themselves as a single people, fragile as it may have been, made possible the creation of a loose confederacy of states under the Articles of Confederation in 1781–89 and an even more unified federal government under the Constitution in 1789.

The Articles of Confederation was the first governing document of the United States, but it gave little power to Congress and did not include an executive or judiciary branch. National Archives, Washington, D.C.

Because of the new country's large population and enormous size, it was obvious to the delegates to the Constitutional Convention (1787) that "the People of the United States," as the opening words of the Constitution referred to them, could govern themselves at the federal level only by electing representatives—a practice with which the delegates were already familiar, given their experience of state government and, more remotely, their dealings with the government in Britain. The new representative government was barely in place, however, when it became evident that the task of organizing members of Congress and the electorate required the existence of political parties, even though such parties had been regarded as pernicious and destructive—"the bane of republics"—by political thinkers and by many delegates to the Constitutional Convention. Eventually, political parties in the United States would provide nominees for local, state, and national offices and compete openly and vigorously in elections.

It was also obvious that a country as large as the United States would require representative government at lower levels (e.g., territories, states, and municipalities) with correspondingly limited powers. Although the governments of territories and states were necessarily representative, in smaller associations a direct assembly of citizens was both feasible and desirable. In many New England towns, for example, citizens assembled in meetings, Athenian style, to discuss and vote on local matters.

Thus, the citizens of the United States helped to provide new answers to question (1)—What is the appropriate unit or association within which a democratic government should be established?—and question (3)—How are citizens to govern? Yet, the American answer to question (2)—Who should constitute the *dēmos*?—though radical in its time, was by later standards highly unsatisfactory. Even as the suffrage was broadly extended among adult white males, it continued to exclude large segments of the adult population, such as women, slaves, many freed blacks, and Native Americans. In

Thomas Jefferson

Thomas Jefferson was born on April 2 (April 13, New Style), 1743, in Shadwell, Va. (U.S.), and died on July 4, 1826, in Monticello, Va. Jefferson was a draftsman of the Declaration of Independence of the United States and the nation's first secretary of state (1789–94), second vice president (1797–1801), and, as the third president (1801–09), the statesman responsible for the Louisiana Purchase. An early advocate of total separation of church and state, he also was the founder and architect of the University of Virginia and the most eloquent American proponent of individual freedom as the core meaning of the American Revolution.

Long regarded as America's most distinguished "apostle of liberty," Jefferson has come under increasingly critical scrutiny within the scholarly world. At the popular level, both in the United States and abroad, he remains an incandescent icon, an inspirational symbol for both major U.S. political parties, as well as for dissenters in communist China, liberal reformers in central and eastern Europe, and aspiring democrats in Africa and Latin America. His image within scholarly circles has suffered, however, as the focus on racial equality has prompted a more negative reappraisal of his dependence upon slavery and his conviction that American society remain a white man's domain. The huge gap between his lyrical expression of liberal ideals and the more attenuated reality of his own life has transformed Jefferson into America's most problematic and paradoxical hero. The Jefferson Memorial in Washington, D.C., was dedicated to him on April 13, 1943, the 200th anniversary of his birth.

time, these exclusions, like those of earlier democracies and republics, would be widely regarded as undemocratic.

Articles of Confederation

The Articles of Confederation were the first U.S. constitution (1781–89), which served as a bridge between the initial government by the Continental Congress of the Revolutionary period and the federal government provided under the U.S. Constitution of 1787. Because the experience of overbearing British central authority was vivid in colonial minds, the drafters of the Articles deliberately established a confederation of sovereign states. The Articles were written in 1776–77 and adopted by the Congress on Nov. 15, 1777. However, the document was not fully ratified by the states until March 1, 1781.

On paper, the Congress had power to regulate foreign affairs, war, and the postal service and to appoint military officers, control Indian affairs, borrow money, determine the

Independence Hall in Philadelphia, Pa., was the setting for the debate and adoption of the Declaration of Independence, Articles of Confederation, and U.S. Constitution. Allyn Cox, Architect of the Capitol

value of coin, and issue bills of credit. In reality, however, the Articles gave the Congress no power to enforce its requests to the states for money or troops, and by the end of 1786 governmental effectiveness had broken down.

Nevertheless, some solid accomplishments had been achieved: certain state claims to western lands were settled, and the Northwest Ordinance of 1787 established the fundamental pattern of evolving government in the territories north of the Ohio River. Equally important, the

James Madison

James Madison, in full James Madison, Jr., was born on March 16, 1751, in Port Conway, Va., and died on June 28, 1836, in Montpelier, Va. He was the fourth president of the United States (1809–17) and one of the Founding Fathers of his country. At the Constitutional Convention (1787), he influenced the planning and ratification of the U.S. Constitution and collaborated with Alexander Hamilton and John Jay in the publication of the Federalist papers. As a member of the new House of Representatives, he sponsored the first 10 amendments to the Constitution, commonly called the Bill of Rights. He was secretary of state under Pres. Thomas Jefferson when the Louisiana Territory was purchased from France. The War of 1812 was fought during his presidency.

Madison took day-by-day notes of debates at the Constitutional Convention, which furnish the only comprehensive history of the proceedings. To promote ratification he collaborated with Alexander Hamilton and John Jay in newspaper publication of the Federalist papers (Madison wrote 29 out of 85), which became the standard commentary on the Constitution. His influence produced ratification by Virginia and led John Marshall to say that, if eloquence included "persuasion by convincing, Mr. Madison was the most eloquent man I ever heard."

Confederation provided the new nation with instructive experience in self-government under a written document. In revealing their own weaknesses, the Articles paved the way for the Constitutional Convention of 1787 and the present form of U.S. government.

Constitution of the United States of America

In short, the Constitution of the United States is the fundamental law of the U.S. federal system of government and a landmark document of the Western world. The oldest written national constitution in use, the Constitution defines the principal organs of government and their jurisdictions and the basic rights of citizens.

Constitutional Convention

The Constitution was written during the summer of 1787 in Philadelphia, Pa., by 55 delegates to a Constitutional Convention that was called ostensibly to amend the Articles of Confederation (1781–89), the country's first written constitution. The Constitution was the product of political compromise after long and often rancorous debates over issues such as states' rights, representation, and slavery. Delegates from small and large states disagreed over whether the number of representatives in the new federal legislature should be the same for each state—as was the case under the Articles of Confederation—or different depending on a state's population. In addition, some delegates from Northern states sought to abolish slavery or, failing that, to make representation dependent on the size of a state's free population. At the same time, some Southern delegates threatened to abandon the convention if their demands to keep slavery and the slave trade legal and to count slaves for representation purposes were not met.

Eventually the framers resolved their disputes by adopting a proposal put forward by the Connecticut delegation. The Great Compromise, as it came to be known, created a bicameral legislature with a Senate, in which all states would be equally represented, and a House of Representatives, in which representation would be apportioned on the basis of a state's free population plus three-fifths of its slave population. (The inclusion of the slave population was known separately as the three-fifths compromise.) A further compromise on slavery prohibited Congress from banning the importation of slaves until 1808 (Article I, Section 9). After all the disagreements were bridged, the new Constitution was submitted for ratification to the 13 states on Sept. 28, 1787. In 1787–88, in an effort to persuade New York to ratify the Constitution, Alexander Hamilton, John Jay, and James Madison published a series of essays on the Constitution and republican government in New York newspapers. Their work, written under the pseudonym "Publius" and collected and published in book form as *The Federalist* (1788), became a classic exposition and defense of the Constitution.

In June 1788, after the Constitution had been ratified by nine states (as required by Article VII), Congress set March 4, 1789, as the date for the new government to commence proceedings (the first elections under the Constitution were held late in 1788). Because ratification in many states was contingent on the promised addition of a Bill of Rights, Congress proposed 12 amendments in September 1789; 10 were ratified by the states, and their adoption was certified on Dec. 15, 1791. (One of the original 12 proposed amendments, which prohibited midterm changes in compensation for members of Congress, was ratified in 1992 as the Twenty-seventh Amendment. The last one, concerning the ratio of

Representation

In government, representation is the method or process of enabling the citizenry, or some of them, to participate in the shaping of legislation and governmental policy through deputies chosen by them.

The rationale of representative government is that in large modern countries the people cannot all assemble, as they did in the marketplace of democratic Athens or Rome; and if, therefore, the people are to participate in government, they must select and elect a small number from among themselves to represent and to act for them. In modern polities with large populations, representation in some form is necessary if government is to be based on the consent of the governed. Elected representatives are also less likely to reflect the transitory political passions of the moment than are the people, and thus they provide greater stability and continuity of policy to a government.

Through the course of long historical evolution, various methods and devices have been developed in attempts to solve the many problems that have arisen in connection with representation. These problems include the qualifications of electors; the apportionment of constituencies; apportionment (electoral); the basis of election; methods of nominating candidates; and means of ascertaining the wishes of electors. Because of the need to formulate systematically the demands of citizens, political parties have come to act as intermediaries between the citizens and their representatives. Political debate along party lines has thus become a characteristic feature of most representative systems of government.

How answerable a representative should be to his electors is an issue that has long been debated. The basic alternatives are that the representatives of the people act as delegates carrying out instructions or that they are free agents, acting in accordance with their best ability and understanding.

The representative principle is not limited to government: it is applied in electing executive officers of large social organizations such as trade unions and professional associations.

citizens per member of the House of Representatives, has never been adopted.)

The authors of the Constitution were heavily influenced by the country's experience under the Articles of Confederation, which had attempted to retain as much independence and sovereignty for the states as possible and to assign to the central government only those nationally important functions that the states could not handle individually. But the events of the years 1781 to 1787, including the national government's inability to act during Shays's Rebellion (1786–87) in Massachusetts, showed that the Articles were unworkable because they deprived the national government of many essential powers, including direct taxation and the ability to regulate interstate commerce. It was hoped that the new Constitution would remedy this problem.

The framers of the Constitution were especially concerned with limiting the power of government and securing the liberty of citizens. The doctrine of legislative, executive, and judicial separation of powers, the checks and balances of each branch against the others, and the explicit guarantees of individual liberty were all designed to strike a balance between authority and liberty—the central purpose of American constitutional law.

Provisions

The Constitution concisely organizes the country's basic political institutions. The main text comprises seven articles. Article I vests all legislative powers in the Congress—the House of Representatives and the Senate. The Great Compromise stipulated that representation in the House would be based on population, and each state is entitled to two senators. Members of the House serve terms of two years, senators terms of six. Among the powers delegated to Congress are the right to levy taxes, borrow money, regulate interstate commerce, provide for military forces, declare war, and determine member seating and rules of procedure. The House initiates impeachment proceedings, and the Senate adjudicates them.

Article II vests executive power in the office of the presidency of the United States. The president, selected by an electoral college to serve a four-year term, is given responsibilities common to chief executives, including serving as commander in chief of the armed forces, negotiating treaties (two-thirds of the Senate must concur), and granting pardons. The president's vast appointment powers, which include members of the federal judiciary and the cabinet, are subject to the "advice and consent" (majority approval) of the Senate (Article II, Section 2). Originally presidents were eligible for continual reelection, but the Twenty-second Amendment (1951) later prohibited any person from being elected president more than twice. Although the formal powers of the president are constitutionally quite limited and vague in comparison with those of the Congress, a variety of historical and technological factors—such as the centralization of power in the executive branch during war and the advent of television—have increased the informal responsibilities of the office extensively to embrace other aspects of political leadership, including proposing legislation to Congress.

Article III places judicial power in the hands of the courts. The Constitution is interpreted by the courts, and the Supreme Court of the United States is the final court of appeal from the state and lower federal courts. The power of American courts to rule on the constitutionality of laws, known as judicial review, is held by few other courts in the world and is not explicitly granted in the Constitution. The principle of judicial review was first asserted by Supreme Court Chief Justice John Marshall in *Marbury v. Madison* (1803), when the court ruled that it had the authority to void national or state laws.

Beyond the body of judicial rulings interpreting it, the Constitution acquires meaning in a broader sense at the hands of all who use it. Congress on innumerable occasions has given new scope to the document through statutes, such as those creating executive departments, the federal courts, territories, and states; controlling succession to the presidency; and setting up the executive budget system. The chief executive also has contributed to constitutional interpretation, as in the development of the executive agreement as an instrument of foreign policy. Practices outside the letter of the Constitution based on custom and usage are often recognized as constitutional elements; they include the system of political parties, presidential nomination procedures, and the conduct of election campaigns. The presidential cabinet is largely a constitutional "convention" based on custom, and the actual operation of the electoral college system is also a convention.

Article IV deals, in part, with relations between the states and privileges of the citizens of the states. These provisions include the full faith and credit clause, which requires states to recognize the official acts and judicial proceedings of other states; the requirement that each state provide citizens from other states with all the privileges and immunities afforded the citizens of that state; and the guarantee of a republican form of government for each state.

Article V stipulates the procedures for amending the Constitution. Amendments may be proposed by a two-thirds vote of both houses of Congress or by a convention called by Congress on the application of the legislatures of two-thirds of the states. Proposed amendments must be ratified by three-fourths of the state legislatures or by conventions in as many states, depending on the decision of Congress. All subsequent amendments have been proposed by Congress, and all but one—the Twenty-first Amendment, which repealed prohibition (the Eighteenth Amendment)—have been ratified by state legislatures.

Article VI, which prohibits religious tests for officeholders, also deals with public debts and the supremacy of the Constitution, citing the document as "the supreme Law of the Land;...any Thing in the Constitution or Laws of any State to the Contrary notwithstanding." Article VII stipulated that the Constitution would become operational after being ratified by nine states.

The national government has only those constitutional powers that are delegated to it either expressly or by implication; the states, unless otherwise restricted, possess all the remaining powers (Tenth Amendment). Thus, national powers are enumerated (Article I, Section 8, paragraphs 1–17), and state powers are not. The state powers are often called residual, or reserved, powers. The elastic, or necessary and proper, clause (Article I, Section 8, paragraph 18) states that Congress shall have the authority "To make all Laws which shall be necessary and proper for carrying into Execution" the various powers vested in the national government. Thus, it follows that, in addition to the delegated powers, Congress possesses implied powers, a proposition established by Chief Justice Marshall in *McCulloch v. Maryland* (1819). The issue of national versus state power was not fully resolved by this decision, however, and many political battles in American history—including debates on nullification, slavery, racial segregation, and abortion—often have been disputes over constitutional interpretations of implied and residual powers.

Competing concepts of federal supremacy and states' rights were brought into sharp relief in questions about commercial regulation. The commerce clause simply authorized Congress "To regulate Commerce with foreign Nations, and among the several States, and with the Indian Tribes." Particularly since a series of decisions in 1937, the court has interpreted Congress's regulatory power broadly under the commerce clause as new methods of interstate transportation and communication have come into use. States may not regulate any aspect of interstate commerce that Congress has preempted.

John Marshall

John Marshall was born on Sept. 24, 1755, near Germantown (now Midland), Va., and died on July 6, 1835, in Philadelphia, Pa. He became the fourth chief justice of the United States and a principal founder of the U.S. system of constitutional law. As perhaps the Supreme Court's most influential chief justice, Marshall was responsible for constructing and defending both the foundation of judicial power and the principles of American federalism. The first of his great cases in more than 30 years of service was *Marbury v. Madison* (1803), which established the Supreme Court's right to expound constitutional law and exercise judicial review by declaring laws unconstitutional. His defense of federalism was articulated in *McCulloch v. Maryland* (1819), which upheld the authority of Congress to create the Bank of the United States and declared unconstitutional the right of a state to tax an instrument of the federal government. In his ruling on *McCulloch*, Marshall at once explained the authority of the court to interpret the constitution, the nature of federal-state relations inherent in a federal system of government, and the democratic nature of both the U.S. government and its governing. During his tenure as chief justice, Marshall participated in more than 1,000 decisions, writing more than 500 of them himself.

Civil Liberties and the Bill of Rights

The federal government is obliged by many constitutional provisions to respect the individual citizen's basic rights. Some civil liberties were specified in the original document, notably in the provisions guaranteeing the writ of habeas corpus and trial by jury in criminal cases (Article III, Section 2) and forbidding bills of attainder and ex post facto laws (Article I, Section 9). But the most significant limitations to government's power over the individual were added in 1791 in the Bill of Rights—which is made up of the first 10 amendments to the U.S. Constitution. The Constitution's First Amendment guarantees the rights of conscience, such as freedom of religion, speech, and the press, and the right of peaceful assembly and petition. Other guarantees in the Bill of Rights require fair procedures for persons accused of a crime—such as protection against unreasonable search and seizure, compulsory self-incrimination, double jeopardy, and excessive bail—and guarantees of a speedy and public trial by a local, impartial jury before an impartial judge and representation by counsel. Rights of private property are also guaranteed. Although the Bill of Rights is a broad expression of individual civil liberties, the ambiguous wording of many of its provisions—such as the Second Amendment's right "to keep and bear arms" and the Eighth Amendment's prohibition of "cruel and unusual punishments"—has been a source of constitutional controversy and intense political debate. Further, the rights guaranteed are not absolute, and there has been considerable disagreement about the extent to which they limit governmental authority. The Bill of Rights originally protected citizens only from the national government. For example, although the Constitution prohibited the establishment of an official religion at the national level, the official state-supported religion of Massachusetts was

Congregationalism until 1833. Thus, individual citizens had to look to state constitutions for protection of their rights against state governments.

The Fourteenth Amendment

After the American Civil War, three new constitutional amendments were adopted: the Thirteenth, which abolished slavery; the Fourteenth, which granted citizenship to former slaves; and the Fifteenth, which guaranteed former male slaves the right to vote. The Fourteenth Amendment placed an important federal limitation on the states by forbidding them to deny to any person "life, liberty, or property, without due process of law" and guaranteeing every person within a state's jurisdiction "the equal protection of its laws." Later interpretations by the Supreme Court in the 20th century gave these two clauses added significance. In *Gitlow v. New York* (1925), the due process clause was interpreted by the Supreme Court to broaden the applicability of the Bill of Rights' protection of speech to the states, holding both levels of government to the same constitutional standard. During subsequent decades, the Supreme Court selectively applied the due process clause to protect other liberties guaranteed in the Bill of Rights, including freedom of religion and the press and guarantees of a fair trial, including the defendant's right to an impartial judge and the assistance of counsel. Most controversial was the Supreme Court's application of this due process clause to the *Roe v. Wade* case, which led to the legalization of abortion in 1973.

The Supreme Court applied the equal protection clause of the Fourteenth Amendment in its landmark decision in *Brown v. Board of Education of Topeka* (1954), in which it ruled that racial segregation in public schools was unconstitutional. In the 1960s and '70s the equal protection clause was used by the Supreme Court to extend protections to other areas, including zoning laws, voting rights, and gender discrimination. The broad interpretation of this clause has also caused considerable controversy.

The Constitution as a Living Document

Twenty-seven amendments have been added to the Constitution since 1789. In addition to those mentioned previously, other far-reaching amendments include the Sixteenth (1913), which allowed Congress to impose an income tax; the Seventeenth (1913), which provided for direct election of senators; the Nineteenth (1920), which mandated women's suffrage; and the Twenty-sixth (1971), which granted suffrage to citizens 18 years of age and older.

In more than two centuries of operation, the United States Constitution has proved itself a dynamic document. It has served as a model for other countries, its provisions being widely imitated in national constitutions throughout the world. Although the Constitution's brevity and ambiguity have sometimes led to serious disputes about its meaning, they also have made it adaptable to changing historical circumstances and ensured its relevance in ages far removed from the one in which it was written.

Democracy or Republic?

Is *democracy* the most appropriate name for a large-scale representative system such as that of the early United States? At the end of the 18th century, the history of the terms whose literal meaning is "rule by the people"—*democracy* and *republic*—left the answer unclear. Both terms had been applied to the assembly-based systems of Greece and Rome, though neither system assigned legislative powers to representatives elected by members of the *dēmos*. Even after Roman citizenship was expanded beyond the city itself and increasing numbers of citizens were prevented from participating in government by the time, expense, and hardship of travel to the city, the complex Roman system of assemblies was never replaced by a government of representatives— a parliament—elected by all Roman citizens. Venetians also called the government of their famous city a republic, though it was certainly not democratic.

When the members of the United States Constitutional Convention met in 1787, terminology was still unsettled. Not only were *democracy* and *republic* used more or less interchangeably in the colonies, but no established term existed for a representative government "by the people." At the same time, the British system was moving swiftly toward full-fledged parliamentary government. Had the framers of the United States Constitution met two generations later, when their understanding of the constitution of Britain would have been radically different, they might have concluded that the British system required only an expansion of the electorate to realize its full democratic potential. Thus, they might well have adopted a parliamentary form of government.

Embarked as they were on a wholly unprecedented effort to construct a constitutional government for an already large and continuously expanding country, the framers could have had no clear idea of how their experiment would work in practice. Fearful of the destructive power of "factions," for example, they did not foresee that in a country where laws are enacted by representatives chosen by the people in regular and competitive elections, political parties inevitably become fundamentally important institutions.

Given the existing confusion over terminology, it is not surprising that the framers employed various terms to describe the novel government they proposed. A few months after the adjournment of the Constitutional Convention, James Madison, the future fourth president of the United States, proposed a usage that would have lasting influence within the country though little elsewhere. In *Federalist 10*, one of 85 essays by Madison, Alexander Hamilton, and John Jay known collectively as the Federalist papers, Madison defined a "pure democracy" as "a society consisting of a small number of citizens, who assemble and administer the government in person," and a republic as "a government in which the scheme of representation takes place." According to Madison, "The two great points of difference between a democracy and a republic, are: first, the delegation of the government, in the latter, to a small number of citizens elected by the rest; secondly, the greater the number of citizens, and greater sphere of country, over which the latter may be extended." In short, for Madison, *democracy* meant direct democracy, and *republic* meant representative government.

Even among his contemporaries, Madison's refusal to apply the term *democracy* to representative governments, even those based on broad electorates, was aberrant. In November 1787, only two months after the convention had adjourned, James Wilson, one of the signers of the Declaration of Independence, proposed a new classification. "[T]he three species of governments," he wrote, "are the monarchical, aristocratical and democratical. In a monarchy, the supreme power is vested in a single person: in an aristocracy . . . by a body not formed upon the principle of representation, but enjoying their station by descent, or election among themselves, or in right of some personal or territorial qualifications; and lastly, in a democracy, it is inherent in a people, and is exercised by themselves or their representatives." Applying this understanding of democracy to the newly adopted constitution, Wilson asserted that "in its principles, . . . it is purely democratical: varying indeed in its form in order to admit all the advantages, and to exclude all the disadvantages which are incidental to the known and established constitutions of government. But when we take an extensive and accurate view of the streams of power that appear through this great and comprehensive plan . . . we shall be able to trace them to one great and noble source, THE PEOPLE." At the Virginia ratifying convention some months later, John Marshall, the future chief justice of the Supreme Court, declared that the "Constitution provided for 'a well regulated democracy' where no king, or president, could undermine representative government." The political party that he helped to organize and lead in cooperation with Thomas Jefferson, principal author of the Declaration of Independence and future third president of the United States, was named the Democratic-Republican Party; the party adopted its present name, the Democratic Party, in 1844.

Alexis de Tocqueville

Alexis de Tocqueville was born on July 29, 1805, in Paris, France, and died on April 16, 1859, in Cannes. A political scientist, historian, and politician, he was best known for *Democracy in America*, 4 vol. (1835–40), a perceptive analysis of the political and social system of the United States in the early 19th century.

Tocqueville and close friend Gustave de Beaumont spent nine months in the United States during 1831 and 1832, out of which came first their joint book, *On the Penitentiary System in the United States and Its Application in France* (1833); Beaumont's *Marie; or, Slavery in the United States* (1835), on America's race problems; and the first part of Tocqueville's *Democracy in America* (1835–40). On the basis of observations, readings, and discussions with a host of eminent Americans, Tocqueville attempted to penetrate directly to the essentials of American society and to highlight that aspect—equality of conditions—that was most relevant to his own philosophy. Tocqueville's study analyzed the vitality, the excesses, and the potential future of American democracy. Above all, the work was infused with his message that a society, properly organized, could hope to retain liberty in a democratic social order.

The first part of *Democracy in America* won an immediate reputation for its author as a political scientist. During this period, probably the happiest and most optimistic of his life, Tocqueville was named to the Legion of Honour, the Academy of Moral and Political Sciences (1838), and the French Academy (1841). With the prizes and royalties from the book, he even found himself able to rebuild his ancestral chateau in Normandy. Within a few years his book had been published in England, Belgium, Germany, Spain, Hungary, Denmark, and Sweden. Although it was sometimes viewed as having been derived from politically biased sources, it was soon accorded the status of a classic in the United States.

In 1836 Tocqueville married Mary Mottely, an Englishwoman. Tocqueville spent the next four years working on the final portion of *Democracy in America*, which was published in 1840. Its composition took far longer, moved farther afield, and ended far more soberly than Tocqueville originally had intended. American society slid into the background, and Tocqueville attempted to complete a picture of the influence of equality itself on all aspects of modern society. France increasingly became his principal example, and what he saw there altered the tone of his work. He observed the curtailment of liberties by the Liberals, who had come to power in 1830, as well as the growth of state intervention in economic development. Most depressing to him was the increased political apathy and acquiescence of his fellow citizens in this rising paternalism. His chapters on democratic individualism and centralization in *Democracy in America* contained a new warning based on these observations. He argued that a mild, stagnant despotism was the greatest threat to democracy.

Following his visit to the United States in 1831–32, the French political scientist Alexis de Tocqueville asserted in no uncertain terms that the country he had observed was a democracy—indeed, the world's first representative democracy, where the fundamental principle of government was "the sovereignty of the people." Tocqueville's estimation of the American system of government reached a wide audience in Europe and beyond through his monumental four-volume study *Democracy in America* (1835–40).

Federalist Papers

Formally "The Federalist" series of 85 essays on the proposed new Constitution of the United States and on the nature of republican government, the Federalist papers were published between 1787 and 1788 by Alexander Hamilton, James Madison, and John Jay in an effort to persuade New York state voters to support ratification. Seventy-seven of the essays first appeared serially in New York newspapers, were reprinted in most other states, and were published in book form as *The Federalist* on May 28, 1788; the remaining eight papers appeared in New York newspapers between June 14 and August 16.

The authors of the Federalist papers presented a masterly defense of the new federal system and of the major departments in the proposed central government. They also argued that the existing government under the Articles of Confederation, the country's first constitution, was defective and that the proposed Constitution would remedy its weaknesses without endangering the liberties of the people.

As a general treatise on republican government, the Federalist papers are distinguished for their comprehensive analysis of the means by which the ideals of justice, the general welfare, and the rights of individuals could be realized. The authors assumed that the primary political motive of man was self-interest and that men—whether acting individually or collectively—were selfish and only imperfectly rational. The establishment of a republican form of government would not of itself provide protection against such characteristics: the representatives of the people might betray their trust; one segment of the population might oppress another; and both the representatives and the public might give way to passion or caprice. The possibility of good government, they argued, lay in man's capacity to devise political institutions that would compensate for deficiencies in both reason and virtue in the ordinary conduct of politics. This theme was predominant in late 18th-century political thought in America and accounts in part for the elaborate system of checks and balances that was devised in the Constitution.

In one of the most notable essays, *Federalist 10*, Madison rejected the then common belief that republican government was possible only for small states. He argued that stability, liberty, and justice were more likely to be achieved in a large area with a numerous and heterogeneous population. Although frequently interpreted as an attack on majority rule, the essay is in reality a defense of both social, economic, and cultural pluralism and of a composite majority formed by compromise and conciliation. Decision by such a majority, rather than by a monistic one, would be more likely to accord with the proper ends of government. This distinction between a proper and an improper majority typifies the fundamental philosophy of the Federalist papers; republican institutions, including the principle of majority rule, were not considered good in themselves but were good because they constituted the best means for the pursuit of justice and the preservation of liberty.

All the papers appeared over the signature "Publius," and the authorship of some of the papers was once a matter of scholarly dispute. However, computer analysis and historical evidence has led nearly all historians to assign authorship in the following manner: Hamilton wrote

The Federalist papers, written to encourage the state of New York to ratify the Constitution, also explore the broader political question of what constitutes good government. The New York Public Library/Art Resource, NY

numbers 1, 6–9, 11–13, 15–17, 21–36, 59–61, and 65–85; Madison, numbers 10, 14, 18–20, 37–58, and 62–63; and Jay, numbers 2–5 and 64.

Solving the Dilemma

Both the notion and the exercise of democracy had been greatly changed by the end of the 18th century. Political theorists and statesmen could now understand what the Levelers had already seen, that democracy was indeed feasible in the modern era's large nation states by using the nondemocratic practice of representation. Representation, in other words, was the solution to the ancient dilemma between enhancing the ability of political associations to deal with large-scale problems and preserving the opportunity of citizens to participate in government.

To some of those steeped in the older tradition, the union of representation and democracy seemed a marvelous and epochal invention. In the early 19th century the French author Destutt de Tracy, the inventor of the term *idéologie* ("ideology"), insisted that representation had rendered obsolete the doctrines of both Montesquieu and Jean-Jacques Rousseau, both of whom had denied that representative governments could be genuinely democratic. "Representation, or representative government," he wrote, "may be considered as a new invention, unknown in Montesquieu's time. . . . Representative democracy . . . is democracy rendered practicable for a long time and over a great extent of territory." In 1820 the English philosopher James Mill proclaimed "the system of representation" to be "the grand discovery of modern times" in which "the solution of all the difficulties, both speculative and practical, will perhaps be found." One generation later Mill's son, the philosopher John Stuart Mill, concluded in his *Considerations on Representative Government* (1861) that "the ideal type of a perfect government" would be both democratic and representative. Foreshadowing developments that would take place in the 20th century, the *dēmos* of Mill's representative democracy included women.

CHAPTER 7

OLD QUESTIONS BUT FRESH ANSWERS

Revolution in democratic philosophies and institutions was hardly limited to representation. Just as radical were the innovative 19th- and 20th-century solutions being proposed to some fundamental questions. One important development concerned question (2)—Who should constitute the *dēmos*? In the 19th century property requirements for voting were reduced and finally removed.

Suffrage

In the 19th century property stipulations for voting were decreased and ultimately removed. The exclusion of women from the *dēmos* was increasingly challenged—not least by women themselves. Beginning with New Zealand in 1893, more and more countries granted women suffrage and other political rights, and by the mid-20th century women were full and equal members of the *dēmos* in almost all countries that considered themselves democratic—though Switzerland, a pioneer in establishing universal male suffrage in 1848, did not grant women the right to vote in national elections until 1971.

Although the United States granted women the right to vote in 1920, another important exclusion continued for almost half a century: African Americans were prevented, by both legal and illegal means, from voting and other forms of political activity, primarily in the South but also in other areas of the country. Not until after the passage and vigorous enforcement of the Civil Rights Act of 1964 were they at last effectively admitted into the American *dēmos*.

Thus, in the 19th and 20th centuries the *dēmos* was gradually expanded to include all adult citizens. Although important issues remained unsettled—for example, should permanent legal foreign residents of a country be entitled to vote?—such an expanded *dēmos* became a new condition of democracy itself. By the mid-20th century, no system whose *dēmos* did not include all adult citizens could properly be called "democratic."

The Civil Rights Act

The Civil Rights Act (1964) is a comprehensive U.S. legislation intended to end discrimination based on race, colour, religion, or national origin; it is often called the most important U.S. law on civil rights since Reconstruction (1865–77). Title I of the act guarantees equal voting rights by removing registration requirements and procedures biased against minorities and the underprivileged. Title II prohibits segregation or discrimination in places of public accommodation involved in interstate commerce. Title VII bans discrimination by trade unions, schools, or employers involved in interstate commerce or doing business with the federal government. The latter section also applies to discrimination on the basis of sex and established a government agency, the Equal Employment Opportunity Commission (EEOC), to enforce these provisions. The act also calls for the desegregation of public schools (Title IV), broadens the duties of the Civil Rights Commission (Title V), and assures nondiscrimination in the distribution of funds under federally assisted programs (Title VI).

Pres. Lyndon B. Johnson (far right) *discusses civil rights issues with African American leaders, including Martin Luther King, Jr.* (centre), *six months before the Civil Rights Act of 1964 was enacted.* © AP Images

The Civil Rights Act was a highly controversial issue in the United States as soon as it was proposed by Pres. John F. Kennedy in 1963. Although Kennedy was unable to secure passage of the bill in Congress, a stronger version was eventually passed with the urging of his successor, Pres. Lyndon B. Johnson, who signed the bill into law on July 2, 1964, following one of the longest debates in Senate history. White groups opposed to integration with blacks responded to the act with a significant backlash that took the form of protests, increased support for pro-segregation candidates for public office, and some racial violence. The constitutionality of the act was immediately challenged and was upheld by the Supreme Court in the test case *Heart of Atlanta Motel v. U.S.* (1964). The act gave federal law enforcement agencies the power to prevent racial discrimination in employment, voting, and the use of public facilities.

Women's Suffrage

Women were excluded from voting in ancient Greece and Republican Rome, as well as in the few democracies that had emerged in Europe by the end of the 18th century. When the franchise was widened, as it was in the United Kingdom in 1832, women continued to be denied all voting rights. The question of women's voting rights finally became an issue in the 19th century, and the struggle was particularly intense in Great Britain and the United States, but those countries were not the first to grant women the right to vote, at least not on a national basis. By the early years of the 20th century, women had won the right to vote in national elections in New Zealand (1893), Australia (1902), Finland (1906), and Norway (1913). In Sweden and the United States they had voting rights in some local elections.

World War I and its aftermath speeded up the enfranchisement of women in the countries of Europe and elsewhere. In the period 1914–39, women in 28 additional countries acquired either equal voting rights with men

In the early 20th century, women's suffrage activists in Great Britain were often known as suffragettes. This suffragette is advertising for a march supporting her cause. Heritage Images/Hulton Archive/Getty Images

or the right to vote in national elections. Those countries included Soviet Russia (1917); Canada, Germany, Austria, and Poland (1918); Czechoslovakia (1919); the United States and Hungary (1920); Great Britain (1918 and 1928); Burma (Myanmar; 1922); Ecuador (1929); South Africa (1930); Brazil, Uruguay, and Thailand (1932); Turkey and Cuba (1934); and the Philippines (1937). In a number of those countries, women were initially granted the right to vote in municipal or other local elections or perhaps in provincial elections; only later were they granted the right to vote in national elections.

Immediately after World War II, France, Italy, Romania, Yugoslavia, and China were added to the group. Full suffrage for women was introduced in India by the constitution in 1949; in Pakistan women received full voting rights in national elections in 1956. In another decade the total number of countries that had given women the right to vote reached more than 100, partly because nearly all countries that gained independence after World War II guaranteed equal voting rights to men and women in their constitutions. By 1971 Switzerland allowed women to vote in federal and most cantonal elections, and in 1973 women were granted full voting rights in Syria. However, women continue to be denied voting rights in many of the conservative Arab countries bordering the Persian Gulf. The United Nations Convention on the Political Rights of Women, adopted in 1952, provides that "women shall be entitled to vote in all elections on equal terms with men, without any discrimination."

Women's Rights in the United States

From the founding of the United States, women were almost universally excluded from voting. Only when women began to chafe at this restriction, however, was their exclusion made explicit. The movement for women's suffrage started in the early 19th century during the agitation against slavery. Women such as Lucretia Mott showed a keen interest in the antislavery movement and proved to be admirable public speakers. When Elizabeth Cady Stanton joined the antislavery forces, she and Mott agreed that the rights of women, as well as those of slaves, needed redress. In July 1848 they issued a call for a convention to discuss the issue of women's rights; this convention met in Stanton's hometown, Seneca Falls, N.Y., on July 19–20, 1848, and issued a declaration that called for women's suffrage and for the right of women to educational and employment opportunities. It was followed in 1850 by the first national convention of the women's movement, held in Worcester, Mass., by Lucy Stone and a group of prominent Eastern suffragists. Another convention, held in Syracuse, N.Y., in 1852, was the occasion of the first joint venture between Stanton and the dynamic suffragist leader Susan B. Anthony; together these two figures led the American suffragist movement for the next 50 years.

Other women's suffrage conventions were held as the movement gained its first mass strength, but at first no way of extending the vote to women was known except by amendments to the constitutions of the various states. Several attempts were made in this regard after the American Civil War (1861–65), but even though the Territory of Wyoming granted women the right to vote in all elections in 1869, it soon became apparent that an amendment of the federal Constitution would be a preferable plan. Accordingly, the National Woman Suffrage Association was formed in 1869 with the declared object of securing the ballot for women by an amendment to the Constitution. Anthony and Stanton were the leaders of this organization, which held a convention every year for 50 years after its founding. In 1869 another organization, the American Woman Suffrage Association, was founded by Lucy Stone with the aim of securing women's suffrage by obtaining amendments to that effect in the constitutions of the various states. In 1890 the two organizations united under the name National American Woman Suffrage Association and worked together for almost 30 years.

When Wyoming entered the Union in 1890, it became the first state whose constitution accorded women the right to vote. Subsequently, vigorous campaigns were conducted to persuade state legislatures to submit to their voters amendments to state constitutions conferring full suffrage to women in state affairs. Efforts were also made to give women the right to vote in presidential elections and, in some states, the right to vote in municipal and local elections. In the next 25 years various individual states yielded to the movement's demands and enfranchised their women; each such state increased the members of Congress elected partly by women. These members were thus at least partly obliged by the nature of their constituency to vote for a women's suffrage amendment to the United States Constitution. By 1918 women had acquired equal suffrage with men in 15 states.

World War I, and the major role played in it by women in various capacities, broke down most of the remaining opposition to women's suffrage in the United States. Amendments to the federal Constitution concerning women's suffrage had been introduced into Congress in 1878 and 1914, but the 1878 amendment had been overwhelmingly defeated, and the 1914 amendment had narrowly failed to gain even a simple majority of the votes in the House of Representatives and the Senate (a two-thirds majority vote in Congress was needed for the amendment to be sent to the state legislatures for ratification). By 1918, however, both major political parties were committed to women's suffrage, and the amendment was carried by the necessary two-thirds majorities in both the House and Senate in January 1918 and June 1919, respectively.

Vigorous campaigns were then waged to secure ratification of the amendment by two-thirds of the state legislatures, and on Aug. 18, 1920, Tennessee became the 36th state to ratify the amendment. On August 26 the Nineteenth Amendment was proclaimed by the secretary of state as being part of the Constitution of the United States. Women in the United States were enfranchised on an equal basis with men. The text reads as follows:

> The right of citizens of the United States to vote shall not be denied or abridged by the United States or by any State on account of sex.
> Congress shall have power to enforce this article by appropriate legislation.

Factions and Parties

In numerous democracies and republics of the city-states, a partial answer to question (3)—What political institutions are necessary for governing?—was made up of "factions," comprising casual groups as well as structured political parties. Eventually, some countries' representative democracies initiated political parties for choosing candidates for election to parliament as well as forming parliamentary backing for (or resistance to) the prime minister and his cabinet. Nevertheless, at the end of the 18th century leading political theorists such as Montesquieu continued to regard factions as a profound danger to democracies and republics. This view was also common at the United States Constitutional Convention, where many delegates argued that the new government would inevitably be controlled and abused by factions unless there existed a strong system of constitutional checks and balances.

Factions are dangerous, it was argued, for at least two reasons. First, a faction is by definition a group whose interests

Checks and Balances

Checks and balances are a principle of government under which separate branches are empowered to prevent actions by other branches and are induced to share power. Checks and balances are applied primarily in constitutional governments. They are of fundamental importance in tripartite governments, such as that of the United States, which separate powers among legislative, executive, and judicial branches.

The Greek historian Polybius analyzed the ancient Roman mixed constitution under three main divisions: monarchy (represented by the consul); aristocracy (the Senate); and democracy (the people). He greatly influenced later ideas about the separation of powers.

Checks and balances, which modify the separation of powers, may operate under parliamentary systems through exercise of a parliament's prerogative to adopt a no-confidence vote in a government; the government, or cabinet, in turn, ordinarily may dissolve the parliament. The British Parliament is supreme, and laws passed by it are not subject to review by the courts for constitutionality. In France, under the Fifth Republic (1958), a Constitutional Council of nine members (appointed for nine years by the president, Senate, and National Assembly) reviews the constitutionality of legislation. The Federal Republic of Germany combines features of parliamentary systems and of federal systems like that of the United States. It vests the right to declare a law unconstitutional in the Federal Constitutional Court (1951).

are in conflict with the general good. As Madison put it in *Federalist 10*: "By a faction, I understand a number of citizens, whether amounting to a majority or a minority of the whole, who are united and actuated by some common impulse of passion, or of interest, adverse to the rights of other citizens, or to the permanent and aggregate interests of the community." Second, historical experience shows that, prior to the 18th century, the existence of factions in a democracy or republic tended to undermine the stability of its government. The "instability, injustice, and confusion introduced into the public councils" by factionalism, Madison wrote, have been "the mortal diseases under which popular governments have everywhere perished."

Interestingly, Madison used the presumed danger of factions as an argument in favour of adopting the new constitution. Because the United States, in comparison with previous republics, would have many more citizens and vastly more territory, the diversity of interests among its population would be much greater, making the formation of large or powerful factions less likely. Similarly, the exercise of government power by representatives rather than directly by the people would "refine and enlarge the public views, by passing them through the medium of a chosen body of citizens, whose wisdom may best discern the true interest of their country."

As to political parties, Madison soon realized—despite his belief in the essential perniciousness of factions—that in a representative democracy political parties are not only legally possible, necessary, and inevitable, they are also desirable. They were legally possible because of the rights and liberties provided for in the constitution. They were necessary in order to defeat the Federalists, whose centralizing policies Madison, Jefferson, and many others strongly opposed. Because parties were both possible and necessary, they would inevitably be created. Finally, parties were also desirable, because by helping to mobilize voters throughout the country and in the legislative body, they enabled the majority to prevail over the opposition of a minority.

This view came to be shared by political thinkers in other countries in which democratic forms of government were developing. By the end of the 19th century, it was nearly universally accepted that the existence of independent and competitive political parties is an elementary standard that every democracy must meet.

Majority Rule, Minority Rights, Majority Tyranny

Although many were sympathetic to democracy in the 17th century and later, fear of "majority tyranny" remained a predominant theme. The general consensus was that any majority would crush the basic rights of minorities. Property rights were perceived as particularly vulnerable, since presumably any majority of citizens with little or no property would be tempted to infringe the rights of the propertied minority. Such concerns were shared by Madison and other delegates at the Convention and strongly influenced the document they created.

Here too, however, Madison's views changed after reflection on and observation of the emerging American democracy. In a letter of 1833, he wrote, "[E]very friend to Republican government ought to raise his voice against the sweeping denunciation of majority governments as the most tyrannical and intolerable of all governments. . . . [N]o government of human device and human administration can be perfect; . . . the abuses of all other governments have led to the preference of republican government as the best of all governments, because the least imperfect; [and] the vital principle of republican governments is the *lex majoris partis*, the will of the majority."

The fear of factions was eased and finally abandoned after leaders in various democratic countries realized that they could create numerous barriers to unrestrained majority rule, none of which would be clearly inconsistent with basic democratic principles. Thus, they could incorporate a bill of rights into the constitution; require a supermajority of votes—such as two-thirds or three-fourths—for constitutional amendments and other important kinds of legislation; divide the executive, legislative, and judicial powers of government into separate branches; give an independent judiciary the power to declare laws or policies unconstitutional and hence without force of law; adopt constitutional guarantees of significant autonomy for states, provinces, or regions; provide by statute for the decentralization of government to territorial groups such as towns, counties, and cities; or adopt a system of proportional representation, under which the proportion of legislative seats awarded to a party is roughly the same as the proportion of votes cast for the party or its candidates. In such a multiparty system, cabinets are composed of representatives drawn from two or more parties, thus ensuring that minority interests retain a significant voice in government.

Although political theorists continue to disagree about the best means to effect majority rule in democratic systems, it seems evident that majorities cannot legitimately abridge the fundamental rights of citizens. Nor should minorities ever be entitled to prevent the enforcement of laws and policies designed to protect these fundamental rights. In short, because democracy is not only a political system of "rule by the people" but necessarily also a system of rights, a government that infringes these rights is to that extent undemocratic.

Bill of Rights

The Bill of Rights, in the United States, is composed of the first 10 amendments to the U.S. Constitution. They were adopted as a single unit on Dec. 15, 1791, and constitute a

The Bill of Rights was added to the Constitution as the first 10 amendments after state leaders expressed fear that the strong federal government would threaten the people's individual rights. © Comstock/Thinkstock

collection of mutually reinforcing guarantees of individual rights and of limitations on federal and state governments.

The Bill of Rights derives from the Magna Carta (1215), the English Bill of Rights (1689), the colonial struggle against king and Parliament, and a gradually broadening concept of equality among the American people. Virginia's 1776 Declaration of Rights, drafted chiefly by George Mason, was a notable forerunner. Besides being axioms of government, the guarantees in the Bill of Rights have binding legal force. Acts of Congress in conflict with them may be voided by the U.S. Supreme Court when the question of the constitutionality of such acts arises in litigation.

The Constitution in its main body forbids suspension of the writ of habeas corpus except in cases of rebellion or invasion (Article I, Section 9); prohibits state or federal bills of attainder and ex post facto laws (I, 9, 10); requires that all crimes against the United States be tried by jury in the state where committed (III, 2); limits the definition, trial, and punishment of treason (III, 3); prohibits titles of nobility (I, 9) and religious tests for officeholding (VI); guarantees a republican form of government in every state (IV, 4); and assures each citizen the privileges and immunities of the citizens of the several states (IV, 2).

Popular dissatisfaction with the limited guarantees of the main body of the Constitution expressed in the state conventions called to ratify it led to demands and promises that the first Congress of the United States satisfied by submitting to the states 12 amendments. Ten were ratified. (The second of the 12 amendments, which required any change to the rate of compensation for congressional members to take effect only after the subsequent election in the House of Representatives, was ratified as the Twenty-seventh Amendment in 1992.) Individual states being subject to their own bills of rights, these amendments were limited to restraining the federal government. The Senate refused to submit James Madison's amendment (approved by the House of Representatives) protecting religious liberty, freedom of the press, and trial by jury against violation by the states.

Under the First Amendment, Congress can make no law respecting an establishment of religion or prohibiting its free exercise, or abridging freedom of speech or press or the right to assemble and petition for redress of grievances. Hostility to standing armies found expression in a guarantee of the people's right to bear arms and in limitation of the quartering of soldiers in private houses.

The Fourth Amendment secures the people against unreasonable searches and seizures and forbids the issuance of warrants except upon probable cause and directed to specific persons and places. The Fifth Amendment requires grand jury indictment in prosecutions for major crimes and prohibits double jeopardy for a single offense. It provides that no person shall be compelled to testify against himself, forbids the taking of life, liberty, or property without due process of law or the taking of private property for public use without just compensation. By the Sixth Amendment, an accused person is to have a speedy public trial by jury, to be informed of the nature of the accusation, to be confronted with prosecution witnesses, and to have the assistance of counsel. Excessive bail or fines and cruel or unusual punishment are forbidden by the Eighth Amendment. The Ninth Amendment protects unenumerated residual rights of the people, and by the Tenth, powers not delegated to the United States are reserved to the states or the people.

After the Civil War, slavery was abolished, and the Fourteenth Amendment (1868) declared that all persons born or naturalized in the United States and subject to its jurisdiction are citizens thereof. It forbids the states to abridge the privileges or immunities of citizens of the United States, or to deprive any person of life, liberty, or property without due process of law. After 1924 the due process clause was construed by the Supreme Court as guaranteeing that many of the same rights protected from federal violation were also protected from violation by the states. The clause finally made effective the major portion of Madison's unaccepted 1789 proposal.

Separation of Powers

Separation of powers refers to the division of the legislative, executive, and judicial functions of government among separate and independent bodies. Such a separation, it has been argued, limits the possibility of arbitrary excesses by government, since the sanction of all three branches is required for the making, executing, and administering of laws.

The doctrine may be traced to ancient and medieval theories of mixed government, which argued that the processes of government should involve the different elements in society such as monarchic, aristocratic, and democratic interests. The first modern formulation of the doctrine was that of the French writer Montesquieu in *De l'esprit des lois* (1748), although the English philosopher John Locke had earlier argued that legislative power should be divided between king and Parliament.

Montesquieu's argument that liberty is most effectively safeguarded by the separation of powers was inspired by the English constitution, although his interpretation of English political realities has since been disputed. His work was widely influential, most notably in America, where it profoundly influenced the framing of the Constitution. The U.S. Constitution further precluded the concentration of political power by providing staggered terms of office in the key governmental bodies.

Modern constitutional systems show a great variety of arrangements of the legislative, executive, and judicial processes, and the doctrine has consequently lost much of its rigidity and dogmatic purity. In the 20th century, and especially since World War II, governmental involvement in numerous aspects of social and economic life has resulted in an enlargement of the scope of executive power. Some who fear the consequences of this for individual liberty have favoured establishing means of appeal against executive and administrative decisions (for example, through an ombudsman), rather than attempting to reassert the doctrine of the separation of powers.

Legislative

The legislature is the lawmaking branch of a government. Before the advent of legislatures, the law was dictated by monarchs. Early European legislatures include the English Parliament and the Icelandic Althing (founded c. 930). Legislatures may be unicameral or bicameral. Their powers may include passing laws, establishing the government's budget, confirming executive appointments, ratifying treaties, investigating the executive branch, impeaching and removing from office members of the executive and judiciary, and redressing constituents' grievances. Members may be appointed or directly or indirectly elected; they may represent an entire population, particular groups, or territorial subdistricts. In presidential systems, the executive and legislative branches are clearly separated; in parliamentary systems, members of the executive branch are chosen from the legislative membership.

Executive

In politics, the executive is a person or persons constituting the branch of government charged with executing or carrying out the laws and appointing officials, formulating and instituting foreign policy, and providing diplomatic representation. In the United States it refers to a system of checks and balances that keeps the power of the executive more or less equal to that of the judiciary and the legislature.

Judiciary

The judiciary is the branch of government whose task is the authoritative adjudication of controversies over the application of laws in specific situations. Conflicts brought before the judiciary are embodied in cases involving litigants, who may be individuals, groups, legal entities (e.g., corporations), or governments and their agencies.

Conflicts that allege personal or financial harm resulting from violations of law or binding legal agreements between litigants—other than violations legally defined as crimes—produce civil cases. Judicial decisions in civil cases often require the losing or offending party to pay financial compensation to the winner. Crimes produce criminal cases, which are officially defined as conflicts between the state or its citizens and the accused (defendant) rather than as conflicts between the victim of the crime and the defendant. Judicial decisions in criminal cases determine whether the accused is guilty or not guilty. A defendant found guilty is sentenced to punishments, which may involve the payment of a fine, a term of imprisonment, or, in the most serious cases in some legal systems, state-imposed physical mutilation or even death.

Judiciaries also frequently resolve administrative cases, disputes between individuals, groups, or legal entities and government agencies over the application of laws or the implementation of government programs. Most legal systems have incorporated the principle of state sovereignty, whereby governments may not be sued by nonstate litigants without their consent. This principle limits the right of litigants to pursue remedies against government actions. Nevertheless, the right of citizens to be free from the arbitrary, improper, abusive application of laws and government regulations has long been recognized and is the focus of administrative cases.

Legal systems differ in the extent to which their judiciaries handle civil, criminal, and administrative cases. In some, courts hear all three kinds of disputes. In others there are specialized civil, criminal, and administrative courts. Still others have some general and some specialized courts.

In many cases the conflicts that are nominally brought to courts for resolution are uncontested. The majority of civil cases—such as those involving divorce, child custody, or the interpretation of contracts—are settled out of court and never go to trial. The same is true for criminal cases in the United States, where the practice of extrajudicial plea bargaining is used extensively. The different criminal process that characterizes the United Kingdom and civil-law countries makes plea bargaining of the sort practiced in the United States less likely—or even officially impossible. Nevertheless, there is evidence that analogous practices for generating and accepting guilty pleas are common in the United Kingdom and are not unknown in Germany. In cases of plea bargaining the court's function is administrative, limited to officially ratifying and recording the agreement the parties have reached out of court.

When the judiciary does decide a controversy, a body of regulations governs what parties are allowed before the court, what evidence will be admitted, what trial procedure will be followed, and what types of judgments may be rendered. Judicial proceedings involve the participation of a number of people. Although the judge is the central figure, along with the parties to the controversy and the lawyers who represent them, there are other individuals involved, including witnesses, clerks, bailiffs, administrators, and jurors when the proceeding involves a jury.

The stated function of the courts is the authoritative adjudication of controversies over the application of laws in specific situations. However, it is unavoidable that courts also make law and public policy, because judges must exercise at least some measure of discretion in deciding which litigant claims are legally correct or otherwise most appropriate. Lawmaking and policy making by

In a trial, the judge (upper left) *presides over a busy courtroom filled with lawyers, their clients, the jury, and witnesses, among others* David Frazier/ The Image Bank/Getty Images

courts are most evident when powerful national supreme courts (e.g., those in the United States, Germany, and India) exercise their power of judicial review to hold laws or major government actions unconstitutional. They also can occur, however, when judiciaries are behaving as administrators, even when they are merely ratifying agreements reached out of court. Patterns of settlement for suits between employers and employees may be more favourable to employees than formal law would seem to require because they are influenced by de facto changes in the law that may result from the decisions by juries or trial judges who may regularly be more sympathetic to workers. Formal laws regulating child custody or financial settlements in divorce cases can similarly be altered over time as juries process the claims of the litigants before them in persistent ways.

After a court decision has been made, it may or may not require enforcement. In many cases the parties accept the judgment of the court and conform their behaviour to it. In other cases a court must order a party to cease a particular activity. The enforcement of such orders is carried out by the executive branch and may require funding from the legislative branch. The judiciary has been described as the least-dangerous branch of government because it has "neither the purse nor the sword," but, in reality, enforcement of the orders of any government institution depends on the enforcing institution's acceptance of the issuing institution's right to make the ruling and to have it enforced.

Jury

In law, a jury is a panel of citizens who participate in the justice systems of some democracies. There are two main types: the petit (or trial) jury and the grand jury. A petit jury decides the verdict in a court trial, in either a civil or criminal case, whereas a grand jury decides whether someone should be brought to trial on criminal charges. By incorporating ordinary citizens into the justice system, juries act as a safeguard against the abuse of power by the government. The modern system of using juries developed in England in the late Middle Ages and later spread through the British Empire; but today, the jury system is used most in the United States. Petit juries are used in a more limited way in the United Kingdom and some countries of the Commonwealth, such as Australia and Canada. Grand juries are currently used only in the United States.

Although the characteristics and powers of juries vary by country, province, or state, juries tend to have a few basic things in common. Juries consist of laypeople, not professional legal experts such as judges, who are generally recruited from a pool of randomly selected adult citizens. The members meet in secret to deliberate, or to discuss the issues, and to reach a decision by voting. Finally, they do not have to supply the reasons for their decisions.

Throughout the British colonies of North America, including Canada after the French and Indian War, juries were used in both civil and criminal trials. Jury trials were highly regarded by the colonists because they served as a means of preventing enforcement of unpopular British laws.

The United States Constitution of 1789 guaranteed the right to a jury trial in criminal cases. Rights regarding juries were expanded in the Bill of Rights, which was adopted in 1791. The Fifth Amendment guarantees that one cannot be indicted for a serious crime in the federal courts except by a grand jury; the Sixth Amendment provides for jury trials in federal criminal cases; and finally, the Seventh Amendment guarantees the right of a jury trial in all federal civil cases in which the amount of judgment might exceed $20. Most states also allow jury trials in civil cases, and all states have offered jury trials for criminal cases since 1968, when the Supreme Court ruled that this is a constitutional right. In both federal and state courts, it is sometimes possible for defendants to waive the right to a jury trial.

Proportional Representation

Proportional representation refers to an electoral system that seeks to create a representative body that reflects the overall distribution of public support for each political party. Where majority or plurality systems effectively reward strong parties and penalize weak ones by providing the representation of a whole constituency to a single candidate who may have received fewer than half of the votes cast (as is the case, for example, in the United States), proportional representation ensures minority groups a measure of representation proportionate to their electoral support. Systems of proportional representation have been adopted in many countries, including Belgium, Denmark, Finland, Greece, Hungary, Israel, Italy, Luxembourg, Norway, Russia, Spain, Sweden, and Switzerland.

Development and Debates

Advocates for proportional representation argue that an election is like a census of opinion as to how the country should be governed, and only if an assembly represents the full diversity of opinion within a country can its decisions be regarded as legitimate. For example, proponents maintain that the plurality system can produce unrepresentative, minority governments, such as in the United Kingdom, where the two major parties governed the country for the last three decades of the 20th century with little more than 40 percent of the votes. The proportional system also is suggested as a means of redressing the possible anomaly arising under majority or plurality systems whereby a party may win more seats with fewer popular votes than its opponents, as occurred in the British elections of 1951 and February 1974.

Systems of Proportionality

Critics of proportional representation contend that in an election a country is making a decision, and the function of the electoral system is to achieve a consensus rather than a census of opinion. Opponents argue further that, by making it possible for small parties to be represented, proportional representation encourages the formation of splinter parties that can result in weak and unstable government.

Unlike the plurality system, which uses single-member districts, proportional representation systems use multi-member constituencies. Systematic methods of applying proportional representation were first developed in the mid-19th century in Denmark by Carl Andrae and in Britain by Thomas Hare and John Stuart Mill. Methods currently in use include the single-transferable-vote method (STV), the party-list system, and the additional-member system.

Single Transferable Vote

The single transferable vote (STV) has not been widely adopted, being used in national elections in Ireland and Malta, in Australian Senate elections, and in local and European Parliament elections in Northern Ireland. Under STV, voters rank candidates on the ballot in order of preference. In the 1860s Henry Richmond Droop developed a quota (the so-called Droop quota) to determine the number of votes a candidate needed to capture to win election under STV. The quota is calculated by dividing the total number of valid votes cast by the number of seats to be filled plus one, and one is then added to the quotient, which is expressed in the following formula:

$$\text{Quota} = \left(\frac{\text{Total Votes}}{\text{Total Seats} + 1} \right) + 1$$

For example, if 250,000 votes are cast and 4 seats are to be allocated, the quota would equal 250,000 divided by 5, plus 1, or 50,0001. After the first preference votes are counted, any candidate whose votes exceed the quota is elected. Votes received by successful candidates in excess of the quota are transferred to other candidates according to the voters' second preferences. Any surplus among subsequently elected candidates is similarly transferred, and so on, if necessary. If any seats are still vacant, the candidate with the fewest votes is eliminated, and all his ballots are transferred to the voters' second preferences, and so on, until all seats are filled. In this way the results reflect fairly accurately the preferences of the electors and, therefore, their support for both individuals and parties. Although the system provides representation to minor parties, results in STV elections generally have shown that minor centrist parties benefit from the system and minor radical parties are penalized. For example, though the Democratic Left (Daonlathas Clé) and Sinn Féin, the political wing of the Irish Republican Army, received similar shares of the national vote in the Irish general election of 1997, the more centrist Democratic Left won four seats to the Dáil to Sinn Féin's one.

Party-List System

Under the party-list system, the elector votes not for a single candidate but for a list of candidates. Each list generally is submitted by a different party, though an individual can put forward his own list. District magnitude (i.e., the number of members per district) varies from country to country; for example, the Netherlands uses a single national district to elect the 150 members of its Tweede Kamer (Second Chamber), and Chile elects members of its legislature by using two-seat constituencies. The overall proportionality of the system is dependent upon the district magnitude, with higher district magnitudes associated with more proportional results. Each party gets a share of the seats proportional to its share of the votes. There are various alternative rules for achieving this; the two principal ones are the largest-remainder rule and the highest-average rule (the latter referred to as the d'Hondt rule, named after Belgian Victor d'Hondt). Under the largest-remainder rule a quota is set, and each party is assigned one seat for each time it meets the quota. These votes are deducted from each party's total, and when no party has enough votes remaining to meet the quota, the remaining seats are assigned on the basis of whatever votes are left. Under the highest-average rule, seats are assigned one at a time to the party with the highest total. After each seat is assigned, the winning party's total is adjusted: The original vote total is divided by the number of seats it has won plus one. Although there are variations, the seats that a party wins generally are assigned to its candidates in the order in which they are named in the list.

Additional-Member System

The additional-member system combines proportionality with the geographic link between a citizen and a member of the legislature characteristic of constituency-based systems. Under this system, adopted by Germany after World War II and in several countries after the fall of communism in eastern Europe, half of the legislature usually is elected through constituency elections and half through proportional representation (the percentage of constituency and proportional representatives varies by country). Each person casts two votes, one for a person and one for a party. In most cases, the party vote is generally used as the basis for determining the overall partisan composition of the legislature.

Trends

During the 1980s and '90s, electoral-reform movements pressed for changes in voting systems. In Britain proportional representation was adopted for elections to the European Parliament and for some local elections in London and Northern Ireland (though not for elections to the House of Commons). Several other countries—notably Italy, which adopted a modified constituency-based system to reduce the number of political parties in the legislature and to create more stability in the cabinet—have altered their national voting systems.

CHAPTER 8

ELECTION

In politics and government, voting is a formal expression of opinion or will that indicates approval or disapproval of a proposal, motion, or candidate for office. An election is the formal process of selecting a person for public office or of accepting or rejecting a political proposition by voting.

In 1994, voters in Johannesburg, black and white alike, line up to cast their ballots for South Africa's first election with universal adult suffrage. © AP Images

History of Elections

Although elections were used in ancient Athens, in Rome, and in the selection of popes and Holy Roman emperors, the origins of elections in the contemporary world lie in the gradual emergence of representative government in Europe and North America beginning in the 17th century. At that time, the holistic notion of representation characteristic of the Middle Ages was transformed into a more individualistic conception, one that made the individual the critical unit to be counted. For example, the British Parliament was no longer seen as representing estates, corporations, and vested interests but was rather perceived as standing for actual human beings. The movement abolishing the so-called "rotten boroughs"—electoral districts of small population controlled by a single person or family— that culminated in the Reform Act of 1832 (one of three major Reform Bills in the 19th century in Britain that expanded the size of the electorate) was a direct consequence of this individualistic conception of representation. Once governments were believed to derive their powers from the consent of the governed and expected to seek that consent regularly, it remained to decide precisely who was to be included among the governed whose consent was necessary. Advocates of full democracy favoured the establishment of universal adult suffrage. Across western Europe and North America, adult male suffrage was ensured almost everywhere by 1920, though women's suffrage was not established until somewhat later (e.g., 1928 in Britain, 1944 in France, 1949 in Belgium, and 1971 in Switzerland).

Although it is common to equate representative government and elections with democracy, and although competitive elections under universal suffrage are one of democracy's defining characteristics, universal suffrage is not a necessary condition of competitive electoral politics. An electorate may be limited by formal legal requirements—as was the case before universal adult suffrage—or it may be limited by the failure of citizens to exercise their right to vote. In many countries with free elections, large numbers of citizens do not cast ballots. For example, in Switzerland and the United States, fewer than half the electorate vote in most elections. Although legal or self-imposed exclusion can dramatically affect public policy and even undermine the legitimacy of a government, it does not preclude decision making by election, provided that voters are given genuine alternatives among which to choose.

During the 18th century, access to the political arena depended largely on membership in an aristocracy, and participation in elections was regulated mainly by local customs and arrangements. Although both the American and French revolutions declared every citizen formally equal to every other, the vote remained an instrument of political power possessed by very few.

Even with the implementation of universal suffrage, the ideal of "one person, one vote" was not achieved in all countries. Systems of plural voting were maintained in some countries, giving certain social groups an electoral advantage. For example, in the United Kingdom, university graduates and owners of businesses in constituencies other than those in which they lived could cast more than one ballot until 1948. Before World War I, both Austria and Prussia had three classes of weighted votes that effectively kept electoral power in the hands of the upper social strata. Until the passage of the Voting Rights Act in 1965 in the United States, legal barriers and intimidation effectively barred most African Americans—especially those in the South—from being able to cast ballots in elections.

During the 19th and 20th centuries, the increased use of competitive mass elections in western Europe had the purpose and effect of institutionalizing the diversity that had existed in the countries of that region. However, mass elections had quite different purposes and consequences under the one-party communist regimes of eastern Europe and the Soviet Union during the period from the end of World War II to 1989–90. Although these governments held elections, the contests were not competitive, as voters usually had only the choice of voting for or against the official candidate. Indeed, elections in these countries were similar to the 19th-century Napoleonic plebiscites, which were intended to demonstrate the unity rather than the diversity of the people. Dissent in eastern Europe could be registered by crossing out the name of the candidate on the ballot, as several million citizens in the Soviet Union did in each election before 1989; however, because secret voting did not exist in these countries, this practice invited reprisals. Nonvoting was another form of protest, especially as local communist activists were under extreme pressure to achieve nearly a 100 percent turnout. Not all elections in eastern Europe followed the Soviet model. For example, in Poland more names appeared on the ballot than there were offices to fill, and some degree of electoral choice was thus provided.

In sub-Saharan Africa, competitive elections based on universal suffrage were introduced in three distinct periods. In the 1950s and '60s, a number of countries held elections following decolonization. Although many of them reverted to authoritarian forms of rule, there were exceptions (e.g., Botswana and Gambia). In the late 1970s, elections were introduced in a smaller number of countries when some military dictatorships were dissolved (e.g., in Ghana and Nigeria) and other countries in Southern Africa underwent decolonization (e.g., Angola, Mozambique, and Zimbabwe). Beginning in the early 1990s, the end of the Cold War and the reduction of military and economic aid from developed countries brought about democratization and competitive elections in more than a dozen African countries, including Benin, Mali, South Africa, and Zambia.

Competitive elections in Latin America also were introduced in phases. In the century after 1828, for example, elections were held in Argentina, Chile, Colombia, and Uruguay, though all but Chile reverted to authoritarianism. Additional countries held elections in the period dating roughly 1943 to 1962, though again many did not retain democratic governments. Beginning in the mid 1970s, competitive elections were introduced gradually throughout most of Latin America.

In Asia, competitive elections were held following the end of World War II, in many cases as a result of decolonization (e.g., India, Indonesia, Malaysia, and the Philippines), though once again the restoration of authoritarianism was commonplace. Beginning in the 1970s, competitive elections were reintroduced in a number of countries, including the Philippines and South Korea. With the exception of Turkey and Israel, competitive elections in the Middle East are rare.

Authoritarian regimes often have used elections as a way to achieve a degree of popular legitimacy. Dictatorships may hold elections in cases where no substantive opposition is remotely feasible (e.g., because opposition forces have been repressed) or when economic factors favour the regime. Even when opposition parties are allowed to participate, they may face intimidation by the government and its allies, which thereby precludes the effective mobilization of potential supporters. In other cases, a regime may postpone an election if there is a significant chance that it will lose. In addition, it has been a common practice of authoritarian regimes to intervene once balloting has begun by intimidating voters (e.g., through physical attacks) and by manipulating the count of votes that have been freely cast.

Functions of Elections

Elections make a fundamental contribution to democratic governance. Because direct democracy—a form of government in which political decisions are made directly by the entire body of qualified citizens—is impractical in most modern societies, democratic government must be conducted through representatives. Elections enable voters to select leaders and to hold them accountable for their performance in office. Accountability can be undermined when elected leaders do not care whether they are reelected or when, for historical or other reasons, one party or coalition is so dominant that there is effectively no choice for voters among alternative candidates, parties, or policies. Nevertheless, the possibility of controlling leaders by requiring them to submit to regular and periodic elections helps to solve the problem of succession in leadership and thus contributes to the continuation of democracy. Moreover, where the electoral process is competitive and forces candidates or parties to expose their records and future intentions to popular scrutiny, elections serve as forums for the discussion of public issues and facilitate the expression of public opinion. Elections thus provide political education for citizens and ensure the responsiveness of democratic governments to the will of the people. They also serve to legitimize the acts of those who wield power, a function that is performed to some extent even by elections that are noncompetitive.

Elections also reinforce the stability and legitimacy of the political community. Like national holidays commemorating common experiences, elections link citizens to each other and thereby confirm the viability of the polity. As a result, elections help to facilitate social and political integration.

Finally, elections serve a self-actualizing purpose by confirming the worth and dignity of individual citizens as human beings. Whatever other needs voters may have, participation in an election serves to reinforce their self-esteem and self-respect. Voting gives people an opportunity to have their say and, through expressing partisanship, to satisfy their need to feel a sense of belonging. Even nonvoting satisfies the need of some people to express their alienation from the political community. For precisely these reasons, the long battle for the right to vote and the demand for equality in electoral participation can be viewed as the manifestation of a profound human craving for personal fulfillment.

Whether held under authoritarian or democratic regimes, elections have a ritualistic aspect. Elections and the campaigns preceding them are dramatic events that are accompanied by rallies, banners, posters, buttons, headlines, and television coverage, all of which call attention to the importance of participation in the event. Candidates, political parties, and interest groups representing diverse objectives

Elizabeth May, a member of Parliament and leader of the Green Party in Canada, speaks to her supporters at a campaign rally. Harald Wolf/Green Party of Canada

invoke the symbols of nationalism or patriotism, reform or revolution, past glory or future promise. Whatever the peculiar national, regional, or local variations, elections are events that, by arousing emotions and channeling them toward collective symbols, break the monotony of daily life and focus attention on the common fate.

Types of Elections

It is important to distinguish between the form and the substance of elections. In some cases, electoral forms are present but the substance of an election is missing, as when voters do not have a free and genuine choice between at least two alternatives. Most countries hold elections in at least the formal sense, but in many of them the elections are not competitive (e.g., all but one party may be forbidden to contest) or the electoral situation is in other respects highly compromised.

Elections of Officeholders

Electorates have only a limited power to determine government policies. Most elections do not directly establish public policy but instead confer on a small group of officials the authority to make policy (through laws and other devices) on behalf of the electorate as a whole.

Political parties are central to the election of officeholders. The selection and nomination of candidates, a vital first stage of the electoral process, generally lies in the hands of political parties; an election serves only as the final process in the recruitment to political office. The party system thus can be regarded as an extension of the electoral process. Political parties provide the pool of talent from which candidates are drawn, and they simplify and direct the electoral choice and mobilize the electorate at the registration and election stage.

The predominance of political parties over the electoral process has not gone unchallenged. For example, some municipalities in the United States and Canada regularly hold nonpartisan elections (in which party affiliations are not formally indicated on ballots) in order to limit the influence of political parties. Nonpartisanship in the United States started as a reform movement in the early 20th century and was intended in part to isolate local politics from politics at the state and national levels. During the last decades of the 20th century, the significance of political parties declined in many democratic countries as "candidate-centred" politics emerged and campaigning and accountability became highly personalized.

Primary Elections

In the United States, a primary election refers to an election to select candidates to run for public office. Primaries may be closed (partisan), allowing only declared party members to vote, or open (nonpartisan), enabling all voters to choose which party's primary they wish to vote in without declaring any party affiliation. Primaries may be direct or indirect. A direct primary, which is now used in some form in all U.S. states, functions as a preliminary election whereby voters decide their party's candidates. In an indirect primary, voters elect delegates who choose the party's candidates at a nominating convention.

Indirect primaries for the presidency of the United States are used in many states. Voters in these elections generally select delegates who attend a national political convention and are bound and pledged to cast their ballots on the basis of the preferences of the voters. Delegates may be bound for only one convention ballot or until they are released by the candidate. In some states, the presidential preference vote is advisory and does not bind the delegates. Rules for selecting delegates are determined by the political parties and vary by state. Delegates can be selected on a winner-take-all basis—as in many Republican Party state primaries, in which the candidate who wins the most votes wins all the delegates at stake—or by proportional representation—as in the Democratic Party primaries, in which any candidate receiving a percentage of the votes above some threshold is entitled to at least one delegate. Allocating delegates by proportional representation makes it difficult for a candidate to build a delegate landslide out of a series of narrow primary victories, and Democratic presidential contests usually have taken longer to select a clear front-runner. In an attempt to enhance the power of Democratic Party leaders and elected officials and to minimize the influence of the primaries, during the 1980s the Democratic Party created so-called "superdelegates," a group of unelected and unpledged delegates that included members of the Democratic National Committee, Democratic governors, and Democratic members of the U.S. House of Representatives and Senate.

The formal, legally regulated primary system is peculiar to the United States. The earliest method for nominating candidates was the caucus, which was adopted in colonial times for local offices and continued into the 19th century for state and national offices. Party conventions were instituted as a means of checking the abuses of the caucus system but also became subject to abuses, which led first to their regulation and ultimately to their elimination for most offices except president and vice president. After 1890, mandatory regulations transformed the primary into an election that is conducted by public officers at public expense.

Although direct primaries were used as early as the 1840s, the primary system came into general use only in the early 20th century. The movement spread so rapidly that by 1917 all but four states had adopted the direct primary for some or all statewide nominations. For the presidential contest, however, primaries fell into disfavour and were generally used in fewer than 20 states until the 1970s, after which most states adopted primaries. Attention from the news media has increased the importance of presidential primaries to the point where success—especially in New Hampshire (which usually has held the first presidential primary) and in other early primaries—gives a candidate a great advantage in publicity and private campaign funding, whereas failure can end a campaign.

The merits of open versus closed primaries have been widely debated. Proponents of open primaries argue that voters should be able to choose which primary they will vote in at each election. Open primaries allow participation by independents unwilling to declare a party affiliation to vote and prevent intimidation of voters who wish to keep their affiliation private. Party organizations prefer closed primaries because they promote party unity and keep those with no allegiance to the party from influencing its choice, as happens in crossover voting, when members of rival parties vote for the weakest candidate in the opposition's primary. Several states have adopted variations, including the mixed primary, which allows independents to vote in either party's primary but requires voters registered with a political party to vote in their own party's primary.

Following legal challenges (particularly by the Democratic and Republican parties), some variations were declared unconstitutional in the early 21st century. For example, for more than six decades, the state of Washington employed a blanket primary, which enabled voters to select one candidate per office irrespective of party affiliation, with the top vote getter from each party advancing to the general election. In 2003 the 9th Circuit U.S. Court of Appeals ruled that Washington's primary was unconstitutional, on the grounds that it violated a political party's First Amendment right to freedom of association. Washington subsequently implemented a modified blanket system that was a nonpartisan contest in which voters could select one candidate per office, with the top two vote getters per office irrespective of party affiliation advancing to the general election; in 2008 this "top-two" system was declared constitutional by the U.S. Supreme Court. In 2010 voters in California, which had earlier also been forced to abandon its blanket primary, endorsed a ballot initiative that established a system similar to that in Washington.

Although the formal primary system is peculiar to the United States, there are some parallels in other countries. For example, the Australian Labor Party has used a "preselection" ballot, in which candidates in each locality have been selected by party members in that locality from those offering themselves for the preselection vote. Some parties in Israel have also used primaries to select candidates for the Knesset.

Recall Elections

Like most populist innovations, the practice of recalling office-holders is an attempt to minimize the influence of political parties on representatives. Widely adopted in the United States, the recall is designed to ensure that an elected official will act in the interests of his constituency rather than in the interests of his political party or according to his own conscience. The actual instrument of recall is usually a letter of resignation signed by the elected representative before assuming office. During the term of office, the letter can be evoked by a quorum of constituents if the representative's performance fails to meet their expectations.

In the United States the recall has been used successfully against various types of officials, including judges, mayors, and even state governors. Although in practice the recall is not used extensively, even in jurisdictions where it is provided for constitutionally, it has been used to remove governors in

North Dakota (1921) and California (2003). Following a bitter partisan fight between Democrats and Republicans over the rights of workers to bargain collectively, Wisconsin experienced in 2011 the single largest recall attempt in U.S. history; six Republicans and three Democrats in the 33-member state Senate faced a recall vote, though only two senators—both Republicans—were defeated.

Referendum and Initiative

The referendum and initiative are elections in which the preferences of the community are assessed on a particular issue; whereas the former are instigated by those in government, the latter are initiated by groups of electors. As forms of direct democracy, such devices reflect a reluctance to entrust full decision-making power to elected representatives. However, because voter turnout in these types of elections often is quite low, voting in referenda and initiatives may be more easily influenced by political parties and interest groups than voting in officeholder elections.

Referenda often are used for bond issues to raise and spend public money, though occasionally they are used to decide certain social or moral issues—such as restrictions on abortion or divorce—on which the elected bodies are deemed to possess no special competence. Referenda may be legislatively binding or merely consultative, but even consultative referenda are likely to be considered legislative mandates. Referenda and initiatives at the national level have been used most heavily in Switzerland, which has held about half the world's national referenda. Evidence from Switzerland has shown that referenda brought to a vote by legislators are more likely to succeed than those initiated by the public. For example, about half of all laws and nearly three-fourths of all constitutional amendments initiated by the Swiss government have been passed, whereas only about one-tenth of all citizen initiatives have been successful. Switzerland uses referenda and initiatives extensively at the local and regional levels as well, as does the United States. Near the end of the 20th century, referenda were employed more frequently around the world than in earlier years; this was particularly true in Europe, where referenda were held to decide public policy on

Plebiscite

Plebiscites are elections held to decide two paramount types of political issues: government legitimacy and the nationality of territories contested between governments. In the former case, the incumbent government, seeking a popular mandate as a basis for legitimacy, employs a plebiscite to establish its right to speak for the nation. Plebiscites of this nature are thought to establish a direct link between the rulers and the ruled; intermediaries such as political parties are bypassed, and for this reason plebiscites are sometimes considered antithetical to pluralism and competitive politics. Following the French Revolution in 1789, the plebiscite was widely popular in France, rooted as it was in the ideas of nationalism and popular sovereignty. In the 20th century, totalitarian regimes have employed plebiscites to legitimize their rule.

Plebiscites also have been used as a device for deciding the nationality of territories. For example, after World War I the League of Nations proposed 11 such plebiscites, the most successful of which was held in 1935 in the Saar, until the end of the war a state of Germany that had been administered by the League for 15 years; its inhabitants chose overwhelmingly to return to Germany rather than to become a part of France. This use of plebiscites, however, is relatively rare because it requires the prior agreement of the governments involved on an issue that is usually very contentious.

voting systems, treaties and peace agreements (e.g., the Treaty on European Union), and social issues.

Electoral System

The electoral system is a method and rules of counting votes to determine the outcome of elections. Winners may be determined by a plurality, a majority (more than 50% of the vote), an extraordinary majority (a percentage of the vote greater than 50%), or unanimity. Candidates for public office may be elected directly or indirectly. Proportional representation is used in some areas to ensure a fairer distribution of legislative seats to constituencies that may be denied representation under the plurality or majority formulas.

Electoral College

The electoral college is the system by which the president and vice president of the United States are chosen. It was devised by the framers of the United States Constitution to provide a method of election that was feasible, desirable, and consistent with a republican form of government.

History and Operation

During most of the Constitutional Convention, presidential selection was vested in the legislature. The electoral college was proposed near the end of the convention by the Committee on Unfinished Parts, chaired by David Brearley of New Jersey, to provide a system that would select the most qualified president and vice president. Historians have suggested a variety of reasons for the adoption of the electoral college, including concerns about the separation of powers and the relationship between the executive and legislative branches, the balance between small and large states, slavery, and the perceived dangers of direct democracy. One supporter of the electoral college, Alexander Hamilton, argued that while it might not be perfect, it was "at least excellent."

Article II, Section 1, of the Constitution stipulated that states could select electors in any manner they desired and in a number equal to their congressional representation (senators plus representatives). (The Twenty-third Amendment, adopted in 1961, provided electoral college representation for Washington, D.C.) The electors would then meet and vote for two people, at least one of whom could not be an inhabitant of their state. Under the original plan, the person receiving the largest number of votes, provided it was a majority of the number of electors, would be elected president, and the person with the second-largest number of votes would become vice president. If no one received a majority, the presidency of the United States would be decided by the House of Representatives, voting by states and choosing from among the top five candidates in the electoral vote. A tie for vice president would be broken by the Senate. Despite the Convention's rejection of a direct popular vote as unwise and unworkable, the initial public reaction to the electoral college system was favourable. The major issue of concern regarding the presidency during the debate over ratification of the Constitution was not the method of selection but the president's unlimited eligibility for reelection.

The development of national political parties toward the end of the 18th century provided the new system with its first major challenge. Informal congressional caucuses, organized along party lines, selected presidential nominees. Electors, chosen by state legislatures mostly on the basis of partisan inclination, were not expected to exercise independent judgment when voting. So strong were partisan loyalties in 1800 that all the Democratic-Republican electors voted for their party's candidates, Thomas Jefferson and Aaron Burr. Since the framers had not anticipated party-line voting and there was no mechanism for indicating a separate choice for president and vice president, the tie had to be broken by the Federalist-controlled House of Representatives. The election of Jefferson after 36 ballots led to the adoption of the Twelfth Amendment in 1804, which specified separate ballots for president and vice president and reduced the number of candidates from which the House could choose from five to three.

The development of political parties coincided with the expansion of popular choice. By 1836 all states selected their electors by direct popular vote except South Carolina, which did so only after the American Civil War. In choosing electors, most states adopted a general-ticket system in which slates of partisan electors were selected on the basis of a statewide vote. Thus, the winner of a state's popular vote would win its entire electoral vote. Only Maine and Nebraska have chosen to deviate from this method, instead allocating electoral votes to the victor in each House district and a two-electoral-vote bonus to the statewide winner. The winner-take-all system generally favoured major parties over minor parties, large states over small states, and cohesive voting groups concentrated in large states over those that were more diffusely dispersed across the country.

Arguments For and Against the Electoral College

One of the most troubling aspects of the electoral college system is the possibility that the winner might not be the candidate with the most popular votes. Three presidents—Rutherford B. Hayes in 1876, Benjamin Harrison in 1888, and

George W. Bush in 2000—were elected with fewer popular votes than their opponents, and Andrew Jackson lost to John Quincy Adams in the House of Representatives after winning a plurality of the popular and electoral vote in 1824. In 18 elections between 1824 and 2000, presidents were elected without popular majorities—including Abraham Lincoln, who won election in 1860 with less than 40 percent of the national vote. During much of the 20th century, however, the effect of the general ticket system was to exaggerate the popular vote, not reverse it. For example, in 1980 Ronald Reagan won just slightly more than 50 percent of the popular vote and 91 percent of the electoral vote; in 1988 George Bush received 53 percent of the popular vote and 79 percent of the electoral vote; and in 1992 and 1996 William J. Clinton won 43 and 49 percent of the popular vote, respectively, and 69 and 70 percent of the electoral vote. Third-party candidates with broad national support are generally penalized in

Newspapers announced George W. Bush's victory on the morning after Election Day in 2000, although the result was not confirmed until a Supreme Court decision five weeks later. Robert King/Hulton Archive/Getty Images

the electoral college—as was Ross Perot, who won 19 percent of the popular vote in 1992 and no electoral votes—though candidates with geographically concentrated support—such as Dixiecrat candidate Strom Thurmond, who won 39 electoral votes in 1948 with just a bit more than 2 percent of the national vote—are occasionally able to win electoral votes.

The divergence between popular and electoral votes indicates some of the principal advantages and disadvantages of the electoral college system. Many who favour the system maintain that it provides presidents with a special federative majority and a broad national mandate for governing, unifying the two major parties across the country and requiring broad geographic support to win the presidency. In addition, they argue that the electoral college protects the interests of small states and sparsely populated areas, which they claim would be ignored if the president was directly elected. Opponents, however, argue that the potential for an undemocratic outcome—in which the winner of the popular vote loses the electoral vote—the bias against third parties and independent candidates, the disincentive for voter turnout in states where one of the parties is clearly dominant, and the possibility of a "faithless" elector who votes for a candidate other than the one to whom he is pledged make the electoral college outmoded and undesirable. Many opponents advocate eliminating the electoral college altogether and replacing it with a direct popular vote. Their position has been buttressed by public opinion polls, which regularly show that Americans prefer a popular vote to the electoral college system. Other possible reforms include a district plan, similar to those used in Maine and Nebraska, which would allocate electoral votes by legislative district rather than at the statewide level; and a proportional plan, which would assign electoral votes on the basis of the percentage of popular votes a candidate received. Supporters of the electoral college contend that its longevity has proven its merit and that previous attempts to reform the system have been unsuccessful.

In 2000 George W. Bush's narrow 271–266 electoral college victory over Al Gore, who won the nationwide popular vote by more than 500,000 votes, prompted renewed calls for the abolition of the electoral college. Doing so, however, would require adopting a constitutional amendment by a two-thirds vote of both chambers of Congress and ratification by three-fourths of the states. Because many smaller states fear that eliminating the electoral college would reduce their electoral influence, adoption of such an amendment is considered difficult and unlikely.

Some advocates of reform, recognizing the enormous constitutional hurdle, instead focused their efforts on passing a so-called National Popular Vote (NPV) bill through state legislatures. State legislatures that enacted the NPV would agree that their state's electoral votes would be cast for the winner of the national popular vote—even if that person was not the winner of the state's popular vote; language in the bill stipulated that it would not take effect until the NPV was passed by states possessing enough electoral votes to determine the winner of the presidential election. By 2010 several states—including Hawaii, Illinois, Maryland, Massachusetts, and New Jersey—had adopted the NPV, and it had been passed in at least one legislative house in more than a dozen other states.

CHAPTER 9

TWO-PARTY SYSTEM

A two-party system is a political system in which the electorate gives its votes largely to only two major parties and in which one or the other party can win a majority in the legislature. The United States is the classic example of a nation with a two-party system. The contrasts between two-party and multiparty systems are often exaggerated. Within each major party in the United States, the Republicans and the Democrats, many factions struggle for power. The presence of divergent interests under a single party canopy masks a process of struggle and compromise that under a multiparty system is out in the open.

Two-Party Inspirations

Major influences favourable to the two-party system are the use of single-member districts for the election of representatives, the presidential system, and the absence of proportional representation. In Great Britain and the United States members of the national representative assemblies are chosen from single-member districts, and the candidate polling the largest number of votes is the winner. Such an electoral system compels a party to strive for a majority of the votes in a district or other electoral area. Usually only two fairly evenly matched parties may successfully compete for office in a single-member district, and a third party suffers recurring defeat unless it can swallow up one of the other parties. Parties do not thrive under the certainty of defeat. A third party may have a substantial popular following and yet capture few seats in the representative body. With, for instance, 20 percent of the popular vote spread evenly over an entire country, such a party would not win a single seat. (Under full proportional representation, it would be entitled to 20 percent of the seats in a legislative body.) The rise of the Labour Party in Great Britain, for example, virtually deprived the Liberal Party of parliamentary seats even when it had a substantial popular following.

In addition to the single-member-district system, in the United States the presidential system induces parties to seek majority support. No fractional party can elect its presidential candidate, and third parties in national politics have proved to be protest movements more than serious electoral enterprises.

The two-party system is said to promote governmental stability because a single party can win a majority in the parliament and govern. In a multiparty country, however, the formation of a government depends on the maintenance of a coalition of parties with enough total strength to form a parliamentary majority. The weakness of the ties that bind the coalition may threaten the continuance of a cabinet in power. The stability shown by the government of the United States has not been entirely due to its party system, it has been argued, but has been promoted also by the fixed tenure and strong constitutional position of the president.

The two-party system moderates the animosities of political strife. To appeal for the support of a majority of voters, a party must present a program sympathetic to the desires of most of the politically active elements of the population. In the formulation of such a program an effort must be made to reconcile the conflicting interests of different sectors of the population. This enables the party, if expedient, to resist demands that it commit itself without reservation to the policies urged by any particular extremist element. In effect, the party is a coalition for the purpose of campaigning for office. In Great Britain and Canada differences in program and in composition between the two major parties have been perhaps greater than in the United States. Nevertheless, in all of these countries a broad area of agreement exists among the leading parties. With two major parties of similar views and of approximately equal strength competing for control of a government, it is possible for governmental control to alternate between the parties without shifts in policy so radical as to incite minorities to resistance.

Systems of Vote Counting

Individual votes are translated into collective decisions by a wide variety of rules of counting that voters and leaders have accepted as legitimate prior to the election. These rules may in principle call for plurality voting, which requires only that the winner have the greatest number of votes; absolute majority voting, which requires that the winner receive more than half the total number of votes; extraordinary majority voting, which requires some higher proportion for the winner (e.g., a two-thirds majority); proportional voting, which requires that a political party receive some threshold to receive representation; or unanimity.

Legislative Elections

A wide variety of electoral systems exist for apportioning legislative seats. In practice, legislative electoral systems can be classified into three broad categories: plurality and majority systems (collectively known as majoritarian systems); proportional systems; and hybrid, or semiproportional, systems. The electoral system is an important variable in explaining public policy decisions because it determines the number of political parties able to receive representation and thereby participate in government.

Plurality and Majority Systems

The plurality system is the simplest means of determining the outcome of an election. To win, a candidate need only poll more votes than any other single opponent; he or she need not, as required by the majority formula, poll more votes than the combined opposition. The more candidates contesting a constituency seat, the greater the probability that the winning candidate will receive only a minority of the votes cast. Countries using the plurality formula for national legislative elections include Canada, Great Britain, India, and the United States. Countries with plurality systems usually have had two main parties.

Under the majority system, the party or candidate winning more than 50 percent of the vote in a constituency is awarded the contested seat. A difficulty in systems with the absolute-majority criterion is that it may not be satisfied in contests in which there are more than two candidates. Several variants of the majority formula have been developed to address this problem. In Australia the alternative, or preferential, vote is used in lower-house elections. Voters rank the candidates on an alternative-preference ballot. If a majority is not achieved by first-preference votes, the weakest candidate is eliminated, and that candidate's votes are redistributed to the other candidates according to the second preference on the ballot. This redistributive process is repeated until one candidate has collected a majority of the votes. In France a double-ballot system is employed for National Assembly

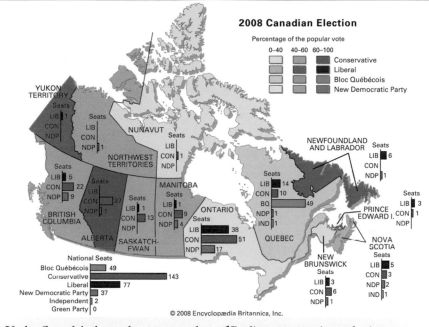

2008 Canadian Election

Percentage of the popular vote

	0–40	40–60	60–100	
				Conservative
				Liberal
				Bloc Québécois
				New Democratic Party

Under Canada's electoral system, members of Parliament can win an election with only a plurality of the popular vote, as the Conservative Party did in 2008 with 37 percent. Encyclopædia Britannica, Inc.

elections. If no candidate secures a majority in the first round of elections, another round is required. In the second round, only those candidates securing the votes of at least one-eighth of the registered electorate in the first round may compete, and the candidate securing a plurality of the popular vote in the second round is declared the winner. Some candidates eligible for the second round withdraw their candidacy and endorse one of the leading candidates. In contrast to the two-party norm of the plurality system, France has what some analysts have called a "two-bloc" system, in which the main parties of the left and the main parties of the right compete against each other in the first round of an election to be the representative of their respective ideological group and then ally with one another to maximize their bloc's representation in the second round. An infrequently used variant is the supplementary-vote system, which was instituted for London mayoral elections. Under this system, voters rank their top two preferences; in the event that no candidate wins a majority of first-preference votes, all ballots not indicating the top two vote getters as either a first or a second choice are discarded, and the combination of first and second preferences is used to determine the winner. Majority formulas usually are applied only within single-member electoral constituencies.

The majority and the plurality formulas do not always distribute legislative seats in proportion to the share of the popular vote won by the competing parties. Both formulas tend to reward the strongest party disproportionately and to handicap weaker parties, though these parties may escape the inequities of the system if their support is regionally concentrated. For example, in national elections in Britain in 2001, the Labour Party captured more than three-fifths of the seats in the House of Commons, even though it won barely two-fifths of the popular vote; in contrast, the Conservative Party won one-fourth of the seats with nearly one-third of the vote. Third-party representation varied considerably; whereas the Liberal Democrats, whose support was spread throughout the country, captured 8 percent of the seats with more than 18 percent of the vote, the Plaid Cymru, whose support is concentrated wholly in Wales, won 0.7 percent of the vote and 0.7 percent of the seats. The plurality formula usually, though not always, distorts the distribution of seats more than the majority system.

Proportional Representation

Proportional representation requires that the distribution of seats broadly be proportional to the distribution of the popular vote among competing political parties. It seeks to overcome the disproportionalities that result from majority and plurality formulas and to create a representative body that reflects the distribution of opinion within the electorate. Because of the use of multimember constituencies in proportional representation, parties with neither a majority nor a plurality of the popular vote can still win legislative representation. Consequentially, the number of political parties represented in the legislature often is large; for example, in Israel there are usually more than 10 parties in the Knesset.

Although approximated in many systems, proportionality can never be perfectly realized. Not surprisingly, the outcomes of proportional systems usually are more proportional than those of plurality or majority systems. Nevertheless, a number of factors can generate disproportional outcomes even under proportional representation. The single most important factor determining the actual proportionality of a proportional system is the "district magnitude"—that is, the number of candidates that an individual constituency elects. The larger the number of seats per electoral district, the more proportional the outcome. A second important factor is the specific formula used to translate votes into seats. There are two basic types of formula: single transferable vote and party-list proportional representation.

Single Transferable Vote

Developed in the 19th century in Denmark and in Britain, the single transferable vote formula—or Hare system, after one of its English developers, Thomas Hare—employs a ballot that allows the voter to rank candidates in order of preference. When the ballots are counted, any candidate receiving the necessary quota of first preference votes—calculated as one plus the number of votes divided by the number of seats plus one—is awarded a seat. In the electoral calculations, votes received by a winning candidate in excess of the quota are transferred to other candidates according to the second preference marked on the ballot. Any candidate who then achieves the necessary quota is also awarded a seat. This process is repeated, with subsequent surpluses also being transferred, until all the remaining seats have been awarded. Five-member constituencies are considered optimal for the operation of the single transferable vote system.

Because it involves the aggregation of ranked preferences, the single transferable vote formula necessitates complex electoral computations. This complexity, as well as the fact that it limits the influence of political parties, probably accounts for its infrequent use; it has been used in Northern Ireland, Ireland, and Malta and in the selection of the Australian and South African senates. The characteristic of the Hare formula that distinguishes it from other proportional representation formulas is its emphasis on candidates, not parties. The party affiliation of the candidates has no bearing on the computations. The success of minor parties varies considerably; small centrist parties usually benefit from the vote transfers, but small extremist parties usually are penalized.

Party-List Proportional Representation

The basic difference between the single transferable vote formula and list systems—which predominate in elections in western Europe and Latin America—is that, in the latter, voters generally choose among party-compiled lists of candidates rather than among individual candidates. Although voters may have some limited choice among individual candidates, electoral computations are made on the basis of party affiliation, and seats are awarded on the basis of party rather than candidate totals. The seats that a party wins are allocated to its candidates in the order in which they appear on the party list. Several types of electoral formulas are used, but there are two main types: largest-average and greatest-remainder formulas.

In the largest-average formula, the available seats are awarded one at a time to the party with the largest average number of votes as determined by dividing the number of votes won by the party by the number of seats the party has been awarded plus a certain integer, depending upon the method used. Each time a party wins a seat, the divisor for that party increases by the same integer, which thus reduces its chances of winning the next seat. Under all methods, the first seat is awarded to the party with the largest absolute number of votes, since, no seats having been allocated, the average vote total as determined by the formula will be largest for this party. Under the d'Hondt method, named after its Belgian inventor, Victor d'Hondt, the average is determined by dividing the number of votes by the number of seats plus one. Thus, after the first seat is awarded, the number of votes won by that party is divided by two (equal to the initial divisor plus one), and similarly for the party awarded the second seat, and so on. Under the so-called Sainte-Laguë method, developed by Andre Sainte-Laguë of France, only odd numbers are used. After a party has won its first seat, its vote total is divided by three; after it wins subsequent seats, the divisor is increased by two. The d'Hondt formula is used in Austria, Belgium, Finland, and the Netherlands, and the Sainte-Laguë method is used in Denmark, Norway, and Sweden.

The d'Hondt formula has a slight tendency to over-reward large parties and to reduce the ability of small parties to gain legislative representation. In contrast, the Sainte-Laguë method reduces the reward to large parties, and it generally has benefited middle-size parties at the expense of both large and small parties. Proposals have been made to divide lists by fractions (e.g., 1.4, 2.5, etc.) rather than integers to provide the most proportional result possible.

The greatest-remainder method first establishes a quota that is necessary for a party to receive representation. Formulas vary, but they are generally some variation of dividing the total vote in the district by the number of seats. The total popular vote won by each party is divided by the quota, and a seat is awarded as many times as the party total contains the full quota. If all the seats are awarded in this manner, the election is complete. However, such an outcome is unlikely. Seats that are not won by full quotas subsequently are awarded to the parties with the largest remainder of votes after the quota has been subtracted from each party's total vote for each seat it was awarded. Seats are distributed sequentially to the parties with the largest remainder until all the district's allocated seats have been awarded.

Minor parties generally fare better under the greatest-remainder formula than under the largest-average formula. The greatest-remainder formula is used in Israel and Luxembourg and for some seats in the Danish Folketing. Prior to 1994 Italy used a special variant of the greatest-remainder formula, called the Imperiali formula, whereby the electoral quota was established by dividing the total popular vote by the number of seats plus two. This modification increased the legislative representation of small parties but led to a greater distortion of the proportional ideal.

The proportionality of outcomes also can be diluted by the imposition of an electoral threshold that requires a political party to exceed some minimum percentage of the vote to receive representation. Designed to limit the political success of small extremist parties, such thresholds can constitute significant obstacles to representation. The threshold varies by country, having been set at 4 percent in Sweden, 5 percent in Germany, and 10 percent in Turkey.

Hybrid Systems

In some countries, the majoritarian and proportional systems are combined into what are called mixed-member proportional or additional-members systems. Although there are a number of variants, all mixed-member proportional systems elect some representatives by proportional representation and the remainder by a nonproportional formula. The classic example of the hybrid system is the German Bundestag, which combines the personal link between representatives and voters with proportionality. The German constitution provides for the election of half the country's parliamentarians by proportional representation and half by simple plurality voting in single-member constituencies. Each voter casts two ballots. The first vote (*Erstimme*) is cast for an individual to represent a constituency (*Wahlkreise*); the candidate receiving the most votes wins the election. The second vote (*Zweitstimme*) is cast for a regional party list. The results of the second vote determine the overall political complexion of the Bundestag. All parties that receive at least 5 percent of the national vote—or win at least three constituencies—are allocated seats on the basis of the percentage of votes that they receive. The votes of parties not receiving representation are reapportioned to the larger parties on the basis of their share of the vote. During the 1990s, a number of countries adopted variants of the German system, including Italy, Japan, New Zealand, and several eastern European countries (e.g., Hungary, Russia, and Ukraine). The British government also adopted a hybrid system for devolved assemblies in Scotland and Wales. One of the chief differences between mixed-member systems is the percentage of seats allocated by proportional and majoritarian methods. For example, in Italy and Japan, respectively, roughly three-fourths and three-fifths of all seats are apportioned through constituency elections.

A country's choice of electoral system, like its conception of representation, generally reflects its particular cultural, social, historical, and political circumstances. Majority or plural methods of voting are most likely to be acceptable in relatively stable political cultures. In such cultures, fluctuations in electoral support from one election to the next reduce polarization and encourage political centrism. Thus, the "winner take all" implications of the majority or plurality formulas are not experienced as unduly deprivational or restrictive. In contrast, proportional representation is more likely to be found in societies with traditional ethnic, linguistic, and religious cleavages or in societies that have experienced class and ideological conflicts.

Executive Elections

Although some executives still attain their position by heredity, most are now elected, though the nature of executive elections

Town Meeting

In the United States, a town meeting refers to an assembly of local qualified voters in whom is vested the governmental authority of a town. Town meetings are a particularly popular form of governmental administration in New England, where a town is a geographic unit, the equivalent of a civil township elsewhere. In New England, towns are granted powers that are granted only to counties elsewhere, as well as their ordinary municipal powers. County government is therefore comparatively insignificant.

At the meetings, which may be held periodically or on demand, officials and school boards may be elected or chosen to govern between meetings; ordinances may be adopted; and taxes and expenditures may be debated and voted upon. Because of the extraordinary autonomy granted each town, New England state legislatures end up being among the largest in the United States.

varies across countries. In the United States, the nation holds a popular vote but the selection of the president is ultimately decided through the electoral college, the majority of which he or she must win. Other nations require a simple majority in order to attain office, though issues such as voter intimidation and corruption call into question the results of some such elections. The nature of nations' electoral institutions thus has fundamental effects on their political representation.

Parliamentary Systems

In most parliamentary systems, the head of government is selected by the legislature. To reduce the influence of minor parties over the formation of governments in the Knesset, in 1992 Israel adopted a unique system that called for the direct election of the prime minister by a plurality vote of the public. Owing to the unanticipated further splintering of the political system, however, legislators later voted to restore their role in selecting the prime minister. Parliamentary systems that have, in addition to a prime minister, a less-powerful nonhereditary president have adopted different methods for his election. For example, in Germany the president is selected by both the upper and the lower chamber of the legislature. By contrast, in Ireland the president is elected by a plurality vote of the public.

Presidential and Semipresidential Systems

In presidential systems and mixed (semipresidential) systems, the head of state is elected independently of the legislature. Several methods of electing presidents have been adopted. In the simplest method, the plurality system, which is used in Mexico and the Philippines, the candidate with the most votes wins election. In France the president is required to win a majority. If no candidate receives a majority of the votes cast in the first round of balloting, the top two candidates from the first round proceed to the second round, which is held two weeks later. This system also has been used in presidential elections in Ghana, Peru, and Russia; Nicaragua adopted a variant of this model that allows a candidate to avoid a runoff with a minimum of 45 percent of the vote in the first round.

Both the plurality and the majority-decision rules are employed in the election of U.S. presidents, who are elected only indirectly by the public. The composition of the electoral college, which actually selects the president, is determined by a plurality vote taken within each state. Although voters choose between the various presidential candidates, they are in effect choosing the electors who will elect the president by means of a majority vote in the electoral college. With the exception of Maine and Nebraska, all of a state's electoral votes (which are equal in number to its seats in Congress) are awarded to the presidential candidate who gains a plurality of the vote in the state election. It is thus possible for a president to be elected with a minority of the popular vote, as happened in the presidential election of 2000, which George W. Bush won with 500,000 fewer popular votes than Al Gore.

Constituencies: Districting and Apportionment

The drawing up of constituencies—the subdivisions of the total electorate that send representatives to the local or central assembly—is inextricably linked with questions about the nature of representation and methods of voting. The problem of electoral representation hinges on the question of what is to be represented. As geographic areas, constituencies often contain within their boundaries diverse, and sometimes incompatible, social, economic, religious, or ethnic interests, all of which seek to be represented.

The solution to this problem has been largely historically determined. Where the interests of electors have not been totally incompatible, and where ethnic, religious, social, and economic differences have been relatively free of passionate conflict, as in the Anglo-American countries, geographic areas (electoral districts) have usually been considered the constituency, and the method of counting has been some system of majority or plurality voting. The elected person represents the whole geographic unit, irrespective of internal divisions. In general, such countries have adopted single-seat constituencies, though multimember constituencies are also possible.

In contrast, where the electorate is composed of several minorities, none of which can hope to obtain a majority, or perhaps not even a plurality sufficiently large to obtain representation, the geographic district can be regarded only as an administrative unit for counting votes. The effective constituency is the group of electors that can be identified as having voted for a given candidate. In this case, election is usually by some method of proportional counting whereby any candidate, party, or group receiving a requisite number of votes is entitled to a proportionate number of representatives.

The drawing up, or delimitation, of electoral districts is linked with differing conceptions of representation, and conceptions of representation in turn are linked with alternative methods of vote counting. Framers of constitutions and advocates of electoral reform have long debated the virtues and vices of different electoral arrangements. Although proportional systems treating electoral districts as merely administrative conveniences and providing for multiple representation are believed to approximate more closely the one person, one vote principle of democratic theory than do single-member

geographic constituencies providing for majority or plurality voting, they are sometimes criticized for contributing to
governmental instability and political stalemate. Critics have
cited the "immobilist" regimes of Weimar Germany (1919–
33), the French Fourth Republic (1946–58), and post–World
War II Italy—all of which had proportional-representation
systems and frequent changes of government—as exam-
ples. Against this, however, there are numerous instances of
politically stable democracies that use proportional representation (e.g., Germany since World War II, the Netherlands,
and Switzerland). In any case, it is doubtful that any other
method of electoral districting and vote counting would be
satisfactory in countries with many interests seeking representation.

Furthermore, representation of geographic constituencies
by majority or plurality voting disguises many differences in the
electorate's composition and preferences. In single-member,
majority-vote electoral districts, the minority that loses at the
polls may feel unrepresented. It is even a precarious assumption that the majority itself is truly represented, as it is likely
to be a loose coalition of diverse interests, and no single representative can usually do justice to the diversity of interests
involved. In general, therefore, the representative, insofar as he
is responsive, is more likely to play the role of broker between
his district's diverse interests than to fill the role of spokesman
for the district as a whole.

Whatever the role of the representative, and however
electoral units are conceived—as geographic areas with stable,
compatible interests or as purely administrative areas for the
purpose of vote counting—districting must be distinguished
from apportionment. In general, if the district is considered
only an administrative unit for counting votes, its boundaries
can be drawn rather arbitrarily without injustice. The district
as such has no stakes of its own to be represented. Conversely,

if the district is considered a true constituency, in the sense that it has unique interests that can be geographically and, as a result, socially defined, districting should not be arbitrary. The area involved should at least be contiguous and compact so that its presumed interests can be fairly recognized.

The difficulty in treating geographic areas as genuine constituencies is that internal transformations in their economic and social structure may make their historical boundaries obsolete. As a result, historical areas serving as electoral districts—such as provinces, states, and counties—may no longer constitute genuine communities of interest to be represented. As these districts become increasingly diverse, it is often difficult to identify particular constituency interests, and representatives find it increasingly impossible to be responsive to constituency wishes or needs.

Problems of apportionment, in contrast to problems of districting, stem from efforts to reconcile the territorial and population bases of representation. If geographic areas, for instance, are assumed to have an equal right to be represented because the area is considered to be a viable constituency, malapportionment in terms of population is inevitable. In the United States, for example, the state of California, with a population of more than 30 million people, has the same number of senators as Wyoming, which has a population of roughly 500,000. This kind of "constitutional malapportionment" must not be confused with the "electoral malapportionment" that defies the one person, one vote principle of equal representation. The latter is usually the result of population shifts.

During the 19th and much of the 20th century, failure to reapportion the number of seats in representative bodies to take account of population changes resulting from increasing urbanization generally benefitted rural electoral districts. More recently, the migration of people from cities to the suburbs has led to possible underrepresentation of suburban populations as against urban ones. From a political rather than a legal perspective, malapportionment is usually considered "undemocratic" because it results in the overrepresentation or underrepresentation of certain sectors of the population and, consequently, may eventuate in public policies not acceptable to the majority of the electorate.

Apportionment is often a complex problem. In particular, it is often unclear how best to define the population among which a specified number of legislative seats are to be apportioned. Any of several distinct quantities—the total population, the number of citizens of voting age, the number of registered voters, or the number of actual voters—may serve as bases of apportionment. If a constant relationship existed between these groupings, apportionment would not be difficult. In practice, however, because of variations in registration and voting turnout, the relationship is not constant.

Constitutional or electoral malapportionment must not be confused with gerrymandering—a form of arbitrary districting used to benefit the party that at a given time controls the apportionment process. Gerrymandering takes its name from the governor of Massachusetts Elbridge Gerry (1744–1814), who recognized the possibility of influencing electoral outcomes by manipulating the boundaries of electoral districts (critics charged that one of the districts he designed resembled a salamander). Gerrymandering involves concentrating large percentages of the opposite party's votes into a few districts and drawing the boundaries of the other districts in such a way that the gerrymandering party wins them all, even though the majority, or, in multiparty elections, the plurality, is relatively small. A widely cited example of gerrymandering occurred in Northern Ireland, where districts were drawn to maximize the representation of Unionists prior to the imposition of direct rule by the British Parliament in 1972.

Gerrymandering is a common political tactic throughout the world. Political parties prefer "safe" districts to those that are competitive. By not contesting seriously in the other party's safe districts, by maintaining one's own safe districts, and by carving competitive districts up in such a way that one's own party is favoured (generally through legislative apportionment), party managers advance their own party's interests but often harm other social, economic, and political interests that need representation. Although gerrymandering is common and generally regarded as legal, gerrymandering based on race has been ruled unconstitutional in the United States.

Voting Practices

There is a direct relationship between the size of an electorate and the formalization and standardization of its voting practices. In very small voting groups, in which political encounters are face-to-face and the members are bound together by ties of friendship or common experience, political discussion is mostly informal and may not even require formal voting because the "sense of the meeting" emerges from the group's deliberations. An issue is discussed until a solution emerges to which all participants can agree or, at least, from which any one participant will not dissent.

By contrast, in modern mass electorates, in which millions of individual votes are aggregated into a collective choice, formalization and standardization of voting practices and vote counting are required to ensure that the outcome is valid, reliable, and legitimate. Validity means that the collective choice in fact expresses the will of the electorate; reliability refers to each vote's being accurately recorded and effectively counted; and legitimacy means that the criteria of validity and reliability have been met, so that the result of the voting is acceptable and provides authoritative guidelines in subsequent political conduct. In some countries that hold elections, observers have reported irregularities in the counting of votes and have questioned the legitimacy of the results. For example, one study of the U.S. presidential election of 2000 found that millions of votes were uncounted as a result of outdated election equipment, registration errors, and other problems, which led some critics to argue that the outcome was illegitimate.

Routinized and standardized electoral practices in mass electorates were developed beginning in the mid-19th century. Their development was as much a corollary of the growth of rapid communication through telephone and telegraph as of the growth of the electorate and rational insistence on making electoral processes fair and equitable. Nevertheless, electoral practices around the world differ a great deal, depending not just on formal institutional arrangements but even more on a country's political culture.

Secret Voting

Once suffrage rights had been extended to masses of voters who, in theory, were assumed to be equal, open voting was no longer tolerable, precisely because it could and often did involve undue influence, ranging from hidden persuasion and bribery to intimidation, coercion, and punishment. Equality, at least in voting, was not something given but something that had to be engineered; the secrecy of the vote was a first and necessary administrative step toward the one person, one vote principle. Equality in voting was possible only if each vote was formally independent of every other vote, and this suggested the need for strict secrecy.

Often called the Australian ballot because of its use in the Australian states of Victoria and South Australia, secret voting gradually was adopted as the norm. Its eventual adoption was largely due to increased literacy and, at the cultural level, to the spread of individualistic norms of privacy and anonymity to certain classes of the population, notably peasants and workers. Traditionally, these groups took their cues from those they accepted as superiors, or from their peers. Secret voting required learning to free oneself as a citizen from customary associations and from pressures for conformity. Even in the contemporary world, developing countries with low literacy rates and with strong ties to tradition were slow to adopt secret voting.

Secret voting dramatically reduces the possibility of undue influence on the voter. Without it, influence can range from the outright purchase of votes to social chastisement or economic sanctions. Although laws exist in most countries to prohibit and punish the purchase or sale of votes, the introduction of secret voting has not wholly eliminated bribery.

Informal social pressures on the voter are probably unavoidable and, in some respects, useful in reducing political rootlessness and contributing to political stability. However, secrecy in voting permits voters to break away from their social moorings and gives them a considerable degree of independence if they wish to take advantage of this electoral freedom. As a result, it becomes ever more difficult for interest groups—whether labour unions, farmers' organizations, commercial or industrial associations, ethnic leadership groups, or even criminal syndicates—to "deliver the vote." The extent to which "deviant voting" occurs depends partly on the degree of rigidity in the social structure. In countries where caste or class barriers are strong or where traditional social, economic, religious, or regional cleavages remain in place, deviant voting is less likely than in countries where there is significant social mobility and where political conflicts cut across traditional social cleavages.

Balloting

The ballot makes secret voting possible. Its initial use seems to have been as a means to reduce irregularities and deception in elections. However, this objective could be achieved only if the ballot was not supplied by the voter himself, as was the case in much early voting by secret ballot, or by political parties, as is still the case in some countries. Ballot procedures differ widely, ranging from marking the names of preferred candidates to crossing out those not preferred or writing in the names of persons who are not formal candidates. Some ballots require the selection of one or more candidates or parties or both, and others require the preferential ordering of a number of candidates.

It is generally believed that the nature of the ballot influences a voter's choice. In jurisdictions where electors are called upon to vote not only for higher offices but also for a multitude of local positions and where the election may include propositions in the nature of referenda, the length of the ballot can affect the results. Overwhelmed by a ballot's length, voters may be discouraged from expressing their preferences for candidates of whom they have not heard, or from deciding on propositions that they do not understand. For example, in some U.S. jurisdictions, participation is often lower in contests for county coroners, tax assessors, and other local positions for which there is often little coverage in the media. Election data show a rapid decline from votes cast for higher offices to those cast for lower offices and referendum-type propositions, a phenomenon referred to as ballot roll-off.

Ballot position also has an effect on the votes cast for particular candidates, especially in the absence of cues as to party affiliation or other identifications. The first position on the ballot may be favoured, and on long ballots both first and

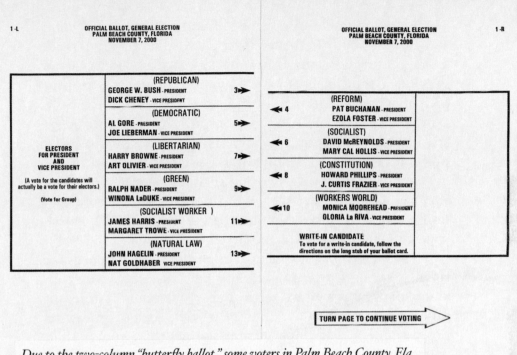

1-L

OFFICIAL BALLOT, GENERAL ELECTION
PALM BEACH COUNTY, FLORIDA
NOVEMBER 7, 2000

ELECTORS
FOR PRESIDENT
AND
VICE PRESIDENT

(A vote for the candidates will
actually be a vote for their electors.)

(Vote for Group)

(REPUBLICAN)
GEORGE W. BUSH · PRESIDENT   3▶
DICK CHENEY · VICE PRESIDENT

(DEMOCRATIC)
AL GORE · PRESIDENT   5▶
JOE LIEBERMAN · VICE PRESIDENT

(LIBERTARIAN)
HARRY BROWNE · PRESIDENT   7▶
ART OLIVIER · VICE PRESIDENT

(GREEN)
RALPH NADER · PRESIDENT   9▶
WINONA LaDUKE · VICE PRESIDENT

(SOCIALIST WORKER)
JAMES HARRIS · PRESIDENT   11▶
MARGARET TROWE · VICE PRESIDENT

(NATURAL LAW)
JOHN HAGELIN · PRESIDENT   13▶
NAT GOLDHABER · VICE PRESIDENT

OFFICIAL BALLOT, GENERAL ELECTION
PALM BEACH COUNTY, FLORIDA
NOVEMBER 7, 2000

1-R

◀ 4   (REFORM)
      PAT BUCHANAN · PRESIDENT
      EZOLA FOSTER · VICE PRESIDENT

◀ 6   (SOCIALIST)
      DAVID McREYNOLDS · PRESIDENT
      MARY CAL HOLLIS · VICE PRESIDENT

◀ 8   (CONSTITUTION)
      HOWARD PHILLIPS · PRESIDENT
      J. CURTIS FRAZIER · VICE PRESIDENT

◀10   (WORKERS WORLD)
      MONICA MOOREHEAD · PRESIDENT
      GLORIA La RIVA · VICE PRESIDENT

WRITE-IN CANDIDATE
To vote for a write-in candidate, follow the
directions on the long stub of your ballot card.

TURN PAGE TO CONTINUE VOTING ▷

Due to the two-column "butterfly ballot," some voters in Palm Beach County, Fla., may have inadvertently voted for Reform Party candidate Pat Buchanan in the 2000 presidential election. Encyclopædia Britannica, Inc.

last names may benefit, with candidates in the middle of the ballot suffering slightly. Ballot position is likely to have its greatest impact in nonpartisan elections, primaries, and elections for minor offices.

The manner in which candidates are listed—by party column or by office bloc—is likely to affect election outcomes. On party-column ballots, it is possible to vote a "straight ticket" for all of a party's candidates by entering a single mark, though voting for individual candidates is usually possible. Conversely, on the office-bloc ballot, voters choose individual candidates grouped by office rather than party, which discourages voting exclusively for members of one party, though some jurisdictions that use the office-bloc ballot allow voters to cast a straight ticket.

Electoral results also can be dramatically affected when some voters find the ballot difficult to use or understand. Indeed, a study in the U.S. state of Florida found that an allegedly confusing ballot design in one county and improperly punched ballots across the state may well have been critical to the overall outcome of the national presidential election in 2000. The analysis, which highlighted the problems associated with various voting methods and the disparate distribution of voting technologies according to socioeconomic status (i.e., wealthier areas generally had more advanced technology and fewer invalidated ballots), spurred extensive debate about election reform.

The type of ballot can have important consequences for the operation of government, especially in systems with separated powers and federal territorial organization. If different offices are controlled by different parties, the governmental process may be marked by greater conflict than would otherwise be the case.

The introduction of voting machines and computer technology has not substantially changed the balloting process, though it generally has made it faster and more economical. Voting machines are not without problems, in that they may marginally depress the level of voting owing to improper use, a problem that can be overcome through improved machines and voter education.

Compulsory Voting

In some countries, notably Australia and Belgium, electoral participation is legally required, and nonvoters can face fines. The concept of compulsory voting reflects a strain in democratic theory in which voting is considered not merely a right but a duty. Its purpose is to ensure the electoral equality of all social groups. However, whether created through laws or

Referendum and Initiative

Referendum and initiative are electoral devices by which voters may express their wishes with regard to government policy or proposed legislation. They exist in a variety of forms.

The referendum may be obligatory or optional. Under the obligatory type, a statute or constitution requires that certain classes of legislative action be referred to a popular vote for approval or rejection. For example, constitutional amendments proposed by legislatures in most of the states of the United States are subject to obligatory referendum. Under the optional (or facultative) referendum, a popular vote on a law passed by the legislature is required whenever petitioned by a specified number of voters. By this means actions of a legislature may be overruled. Obligatory and optional referenda should be distinguished from the voluntary referenda that legislatures submit to the voters to decide an issue or test public opinion.

Through the initiative a specified number of voters may petition to invoke a popular vote on a proposed law or an amendment to a constitution. An initiative may be direct (a proposal supported by the required number of voters is submitted directly to a popular vote for decision) or indirect (the proposal is submitted to the legislature). If an indirect initiative is rejected, the proposition is submitted to a popular vote, sometimes accompanied on the ballot by the legislature's alternative proposal or a statement of the reasons for the rejection. The referendum for constitutional ratification was first used in the state of Massachusetts in 1778. Other forms of referendum and initiative were first used in Swiss cantonal government: the facultative referendum was used in the canton of Sankt Gallen in 1831, the initiative in Vaud in 1845, and the obligatory referendum in its modern form in rural Basel in 1863 (though it had appeared in earlier forms in 1852 and 1854). Both institutions have since been used freely in federal and cantonal matters.

The Swiss experience with the devices of direct legislation was influential in the adoption of the initiative and the optional

(continued on the next page)

referendum in U.S. states and municipalities. The obligatory referendum on amendments to state constitutions proposed by state legislatures was first adopted by Connecticut in 1818 and has become the prevailing method for the amendment of all state constitutions. Some states require a referendum on bond issues; and among local governments, the obligatory referendum is widespread for bond issues, tax questions, and related matters. In the United States, these devices were adopted principally to curb the rule of political party machines and to correct the abuses and inadequacies of inflexible legislatures by granting the people a means to overrule legislative action and to initiate popular votes on legislation.

Although the referendum and the initiative find most widespread use in the United States and the Swiss cantons, they are also provided for in the constitutions of several European and Commonwealth countries. The post–World War II constitutions of France and Italy made popular referenda obligatory for constitutional amendments. In Ireland and Australia, referenda are compulsory for all constitutional change. The constitutions of several states of Africa and Asia incorporate provisions intended to promote closer citizen participation in government, but generally what is called for is not true referendum or initiative, but rather some form of plebiscitary device to support regimes or policies.

through social pressure, it is doubtful that high voter turnout is a good indication of an electorate's capability for intelligent social choice. Conversely, high rates of abstention or differential rates of abstention by different social classes are not necessarily signs of satisfaction with governmental processes and policies and in fact may indicate the contrary.

Electoral Abuses

Corrupt electoral practices are not limited to bribery or voter intimidation. They include disseminating scurrilous rumours and false campaign propaganda, tampering with election machinery by stuffing ballot boxes with fraudulent returns, counting or reporting the vote dishonestly, and disregarding electoral outcomes by incumbent officeholders (e.g., by mobilizing the military to thwart an election loss). The existence of these practices depends more on a population's adherence to political civility and the democratic ethos than on legal prohibitions and sanctions.

The integrity of the electoral process can be maintained by a variety of devices and practices, including a permanent and up-to-date register of voters and procedures designed to make the registration process as simple as possible. In most jurisdictions elections are held on a single day rather than on staggered days. Polling hours in all localities are generally the same, and opening and closing hours are fixed and announced, so that voters have an equal opportunity to participate. Polling stations are operated by presumably disinterested government officials or polling clerks under governmental supervision. Political party agents or party workers are given an opportunity to observe the polling process, which enables them to challenge irregularities and prevent abuses. Efforts are made to maintain order in polling stations, directly through police protection or indirectly through such practices as closing bars and liquor stores. The act of voting itself takes place in voting booths to protect privacy. Votes are counted and often recounted by tellers, who are watched by party workers to ensure an honest count. The transmission of voting results from local polling stations to central election headquarters is safeguarded and checked.

Participation in Elections

Electoral participation rates depend on many factors, including the type of electoral system, the social groupings to which voters belong, the voters' personalities and beliefs, their places of residence, and a host of other idiosyncratic factors.

The level and type of election have a great influence on the rate of electoral participation. Electoral turnout is greater in national than in state or provincial elections, and greater in the latter than in local elections. If local elections are held concurrently with provincial or national elections, generally a higher voter turnout is achieved than for nonconcurrent elections. Whether an election is partisan or nonpartisan also affects turnout, as fewer people participate in nonpartisan elections. Supporters of political parties vote more often than those without a partisan identification. Participation is also usually greater in candidate elections than in noncandidate elections such as referenda. There is evidence that elections based on proportional representation have higher electoral turnouts than majority or plurality elections. Voter turnout tends to be depressed in noncompetitive or safe electoral districts and elevated in competitive ones. The perceived closeness of an electoral contest and the degree of ideological polarization between parties or candidates can affect the competitiveness of the election and consequently its turnout. The frequency of elections is also related to voter participation, as fewer people tend to participate in countries where elections are more frequent.

Technicalities in the electoral law may disenfranchise many potential voters. For example, people who change their legal residence may temporarily lose their vote because of residence requirements for voters in their new electoral district. Complicated voter-registration procedures, combined with a high level of geographic mobility, significantly reduce the size of the active electorate in the United States, whereas in many other countries the size of the electorate is maximized by government-initiated registration immediately prior to an election. Voter registration in the United States is largely left to the initiative of individuals and political parties, though attempts to increase voter registration were made in the 1990s through the implementation of "motor-voter laws," which allowed citizens to register to vote when they received or renewed their driver's licenses.

Relatively low levels of electoral participation are associated with low levels of education, occupational status, and income. Those groups in society that have been most recently enfranchised also tend to vote at lower rates. For a significant period of time in the 20th century, women voted less frequently than men, though the difference had been erased by the end of the century in most countries. The rates of participation of racial minorities are generally lower than those of majority groups, and members of the working class vote less frequently than members of the middle class. In many countries, participation by young people is significantly lower than that of older people.

The failure of certain types of people to vote in elections has important implications. Most analyses have found that if all eligible voters cast ballots, the balance of electoral power would favour the recently enfranchised and less-privileged members of society.

A small group of people are conscientious nonvoters. Others, perceiving the vote more as an instrument of censure than of support, may not vote because they are satisfied with the current government. This group of voluntary nonvoters is also small, however. In fact, nonvoters generally are less satisfied with the political status quo than are voters. The vote is a rather blunt and ineffectual instrument for expressing dissatisfaction, and nonvoting is more likely to be symptomatic of alienation from the political system than of satisfaction with it.

A number of random factors influence individual participation in specific elections. Election campaigns vary in their intensity. A crisis atmosphere may induce a large number of people to vote on one occasion, whereas on another the chance to vote for an extremist candidate may increase the participation of the normally uninterested. Even the weather can affect election turnout.

Voter participation varies from country to country. For example, approximately half of the voting-age population participates in presidential elections in the United States. In contrast, many European countries have participation rates exceeding 80 percent. Even within Europe, however, participation varies significantly. For example, post–World War II Italy has averaged around 90 percent, whereas less than 40 percent of the electorate participates in elections in Switzerland. Research has suggested a long-term decline in turnout at national elections in western democracies since the 1970s; it seems most likely that this is a consequence of partisan dealignment (i.e., a weakening of partisan identification), the erosion of social cleavages based on class and religion, and increasing voter discontent.

Influences on Voting Behaviour

The electoral choices of voters are influenced by a range of factors, especially social-group identity, which helps to forge enduring partisan identification. In addition, voters are to a greater or lesser extent susceptible to the influence of more short-term and contingent factors such as campaign events, issues, and candidate appeals. In particular, the perceived governing competence of candidates and political parties often weighs heavily on voters' choices.

Research suggests that, through partisan dealignment, the proportion of voters in Western democracies who retain their long-term partisan identities has been reduced. In conjunction with the declining impact of social-group influences, voter choice is now more heavily affected by short-term factors relevant to specific election campaigns. This shift from long-term predisposition to short-term evaluation has been facilitated in part by the phenomenon of "cognitive mobilization," a supposed enhancement of the political independence and intelligence of voters who are both better educated and better informed than earlier generations. Nevertheless, many independents and nonvoters are poorly informed politically and relatively uninterested and uninvolved in politics. Whether cognitively mobilized or not, however, independent voters are often a decisive factor in elections. If elections are to be competitive, and if control of the government is to alternate between parties or coalitions of parties, then some voters must switch party support from election to election. New voters and independent voters, therefore, provide a vital source of change in democratic politics.

CHAPTER 10

THE SPREAD OF DEMOCRACY IN THE 20TH CENTURY AND BEYOND

Throughout the 20th century, fewer and fewer countries boasted the fundamental political institutions of representative democracy. As the 21st century developed, impartial onlookers concurred that more than one-third of the world's ostensibly independent countries possessed democratic institutions analogous to those of the English-speaking countries and Continental Europe's more mature democracies. In an additional one-sixth of the world's countries, these institutions, though somewhat defective, nevertheless provided historically high levels of democratic government. Altogether, these democratic and near-democratic countries contained nearly half the world's population. What accounted for this rapid expansion of democratic institutions?

Failures of Nondemocratic Systems

A major part of the reason is that every principal alternate to democracy—no matter what its origins—was affected by political, economic, diplomatic, and military disappointments that made them decidedly less appealing. With the Allied World War I triumph, the early structures of monarchy, aristocracy, and oligarchy were no longer legitimate. Following the military defeat of Italy and Germany in World War II, the newer alternative of fascism was likewise discredited, as was Soviet-style communism after the economic and political collapse of the Soviet Union in 1990–91. Similar failures contributed to the gradual disappearance of military dictatorships in Latin America in the 1980s and '90s.

Expansion of Market Economies

Alterations in economic establishments supplemented these ideological and institutional vicissitudes. Political leaders could take advantage of their access to economic resources to recompense their supporters and penalize their critics, thanks to the highly centralized economies under state control. As these systems were displaced by more decentralized market economies, the power and influence of top government officials declined. In addition, some of the conditions that were essential to the successful functioning of market economies also contributed to the development of democracy: ready access to reliable information, relatively high levels of education, ease of personal movement, and the rule of law. As market economies expanded and as middle classes grew larger and more influential, popular support for such conditions increased, often accompanied by demands for further democratization.

Economic Welfare

Market economies' growth was instrumental to democracy's proliferation in other ways, too. As the economic welfare of sizeable sections of the world's population slowly ameliorated, so too did the probability that newly established democratic institutions would survive and flourish. In general, citizens in democratic countries with persistent poverty are more susceptible to the appeals of antidemocratic demagogues who promise simple and immediate solutions to their country's economic problems. Accordingly, widespread economic prosperity in a country greatly increases the chances that democratic government will succeed, whereas widespread poverty greatly increases the chances that it will fail.

Political Culture

In some countries throughout the 20th century, democracy persisted without being affected by intervals of critical diplomatic, military, economic, or political calamity, like that during the beginning of the Great Depression. The survival of democratic institutions in these countries is attributable in part to the existence in their societies of a culture of widely shared democratic beliefs and values. Such attitudes are acquired early in life from older generations, thus becoming embedded in people's views of themselves, their country, and the world. In countries where democratic culture is weak or absent, as was the case in the Weimar Republic of Germany in the years following World War I, democracy is much more vulnerable, and periods of crisis are more likely to lead to a reversion to a nondemocratic regime.

Present-Day Democratic Systems

Distinctions amid democratic countries in historical experience, scope, and ethnic and religious configuration, just to name a few, have caused noteworthy differences in their political institutions. Following are some of the differences in the features of these institutions.

Presidential Systems and Parliamentary Systems

Varieties of the American presidential system were recurrently espoused in Latin America, Africa, and other areas of the developing world (where the military occasionally used a coup d'état to change the office into a dictatorship). As European countries democratized, however, they embraced forms of the English parliamentary system, which utilized a prime minister responsible to parliament as well as a ceremonial head of state (who might be either a hereditary monarch, as in the Scandinavian countries, the Netherlands, and Spain, or a president chosen by parliament or by another body

Coup d'État

A coup d'état, also called coup, is the sudden, violent overthrow of an existing government by a small group. The chief prerequisite for a coup is control of all or part of the armed forces, the police, and other military elements. Unlike a revolution, which is usually achieved by large numbers of people working for basic social, economic, and political change, a coup is a change in power from the top that merely results in the abrupt replacement of leading government personnel. A coup rarely alters a nation's fundamental social and economic policies, nor does it significantly redistribute power among competing political groups. Among the earliest modern coups were those in which Napoleon overthrew the Directory on Nov. 9, 1799 (18 Brumaire), and in which Louis Napoleon dissolved the assembly of France's Second Republic in 1851. Coups were a regular occurrence in various Latin American nations in the 19th and 20th centuries and in Africa after the countries there gained independence in the 1960s.

convoked specially for the purpose). A notable exception is France, which in its fifth constitution, adopted in 1958, combined its parliamentary system with a presidential one.

Unitary Systems and Federal Systems

In most older European and English-speaking democracies, political authority inheres in the central government, which is constitutionally authorized to determine the limited powers, as well as the geographic boundaries, of subnational associations such as states and regions. Such unitary systems contrast markedly with federal systems, in which authority is constitutionally divided between the central government and the governments of relatively autonomous subnational entities. Democratic countries that have adopted federal systems include—in addition to the United States—Switzerland, Germany, Austria, Spain, Canada, and Australia. The world's most populous democratic country, India, also has a federal system.

Proportional Systems and Winner-Take-All Systems

Electoral arrangements vary enormously. Some democratic countries divide their territories into electoral districts, each of which is entitled to a single seat in the legislature, the seat being won by the candidate who gains the most votes—hence the terms *first past the post* in Britain and *winner take all* in the United States. As critics of this system point out, in districts contested by more than two candidates, it is possible to gain the seat with less than a strict majority of votes (50 percent plus one). As a result, a party that receives only a minority of votes in the entire country could win a majority of seats in the legislature. Systems of proportional representation

In the Knesset, the legislative branch of Israeli government, seats are allocated by proportional representation. A party must receive at least 3.25 percent of the vote in order to win a seat. Gali Tibbon/AFP/Getty Images

are designed to ensure a closer correspondence between the proportion of votes cast for a party and the proportion of seats it receives. With few exceptions, Continental European countries have adopted some form of proportional representation, as have Ireland, Australia, New Zealand, Japan, and South Korea. Winner-take-all systems remain in the United States, Canada, and, for parliamentary elections, in Britain.

Two-Party Systems and Multiparty Systems

Because proportional representation does not favour large parties over smaller ones, as does the winner-take-all system, in countries with proportional representation there are almost always three or more parties represented in the legislature, and a coalition government consisting of two or more parties is ordinarily necessary to win legislative support for the government's policies. Thus the prevalence of proportional representation effectively ensures that coalition governments are the rule in democratic countries; governments consisting of only two parties, such as that of the United States, are extremely rare.

Majoritarian Systems and Consensual Systems

Because of differences in electoral systems and other factors, democratic countries differ with respect to whether laws and policies can be enacted by a single, relatively cohesive party with a legislative majority, as is ordinarily the case in Britain and Japan, or instead require consensus among several parties with diverse views, as in Switzerland, the Netherlands, Sweden, Italy, and elsewhere. Political scientists and others disagree about which of the two types of system, majoritarian or consensual, is more desirable. Critics of consensual systems argue that they allow a minority of citizens to veto policies they dislike and that they make the tasks of forming governments and passing legislation excessively difficult. Supporters contend that consensual arrangements produce comparatively wider public support for government policies and even help to increase the legitimacy and perceived value of democracy itself.

Here again, it appears that a country's basic political institutions need to be tailored to its particular conditions and historical experience. The strongly majoritarian system of Britain would probably be inappropriate in Switzerland, whereas the consensual arrangements of Switzerland or the Netherlands might be less satisfactory in Britain.

CHAPTER 11

20TH-CENTURY THEORIES OF DEMOCRACY

The subject of the democratic state began centuries ago, with Aristotle discussing an ideal democracy. Continuing into the 20th century, scholars have continued to grapple with the meaning of contemporary representative democracy and the expectations to which we should hold governments accountable. The pages that follow explore theories by scholars such as Habermas and Rawls, the value of democracy relative to other political systems, and explorations of the doctrine of liberalism and its proper reach amid changing political circumstances.

Habermas

German philosopher and social theorist Jürgen Habermas, in his series of works published after 1970, used ideas derived from Anglo-American ideas of language to contend that the notion of realizing a "rational consensus" within a group on questions of either fact or value necessitates the presence of what he referred to as an "ideal speech situation." In such a situation, participants would be able to evaluate each other's assertions solely on the basis of reason and evidence in an atmosphere completely free of any nonrational "coercive" influences, including both physical and psychological coercion. Furthermore, all participants would be motivated solely by the desire to obtain a rational consensus, and no time limits on the discussion would be imposed. Although difficult if not impossible to realize in practice, the ideal speech situation can be used as a model of free and open public discussion and a standard against which to evaluate the practices and institutions through which large political questions and issues of public policy are decided in actual democracies.

Rawls

Between the time of John Stuart Mill (1806–1873) and around the middle of the 20th century, the majority of philosophers who argued in favor of democratic ideologies did so mainly on the basis of utilitarian considerations. That is to say, they argued that systems of government that are democratic in character are more likely than other systems to produce a greater amount of happiness (or well-being) for a greater number of people. Such justifications, however, were traditionally vulnerable to the objection that they could be used to support intuitively less-desirable forms of government in which the greater happiness of the majority is achieved by unfairly neglecting the rights and interests of a minority.

In *A Theory of Justice* (1971), the American philosopher John Rawls attempted to develop a nonutilitarian justification of a democratic political order characterized by fairness, equality, and individual rights. Reviving the notion of a social contract, which had been dormant since the 18th century, he imagined a hypothetical situation in which a group of rational individuals are rendered ignorant of all social and economic facts about themselves—including facts about their race, sex, religion, education, intelligence, talents or skills, and even their conception of the "good life"—and then asked to decide what general principles should govern the political institutions under which they live. From behind this "veil of ignorance," Rawls argues, such a

John Rawls is considered the most important political philosopher of the 20th century for his theory of egalitarian liberalism. Frederic Reglain/Gamma-Rapho/Getty Images

group would unanimously reject utilitarian principles—such as "political institutions should aim to maximize the happiness of the greatest number"—because no member of the group could know whether he belonged to a minority whose rights and interests might be neglected under institutions justified on utilitarian grounds. Instead, reason and self-interest would lead the group to adopt principles such as the following: (1) everyone should have a maximum and equal degree of liberty, including all the liberties traditionally associated with democracy; (2) everyone should have an equal opportunity to seek offices and positions that offer greater rewards of wealth, power, status, or other social goods; and (3) the distribution of wealth in society should be such that those who are least well-off are better off than they would be under any other distribution, whether equal or unequal. (Rawls holds that, given certain assumptions about human motivation, some inequality in the distribution of wealth may be necessary to achieve higher levels of productivity. It is therefore possible to imagine unequal distributions of wealth in which those who are least well-off are better off than they would be under an equal distribution.) These principles amount to an egalitarian form of democratic liberalism. Rawls is accordingly regarded as the leading philosophical defender of the modern democratic capitalist welfare state.

Liberalism

Liberalism is a political doctrine that takes protecting and enhancing the freedom of the individual to be the central problem of politics. Liberals typically believe that government is necessary to protect individuals from being harmed by others, but they also recognize that government itself can pose a threat to liberty. As the revolutionary American pamphleteer Thomas Paine expressed it in *Common Sense* (1776), government is at best "a necessary evil." Laws, judges, and

Social Contract

A social contract, in political philosophy, refers to an actual or hypothetical compact, or agreement, between the ruled and their rulers, defining the rights and duties of each. In primeval times, according to the theory, individuals were born into an anarchic state of nature, which was happy or unhappy according to the particular version. They then, by exercising natural reason, formed a society (and a government) by means of a contract among themselves.

Although similar ideas date back to the Greek Sophists, social-contract theories had their greatest currency in the 17th and 18th centuries and are associated with the Englishmen Thomas Hobbes and John Locke and the Frenchman Jean-Jacques Rousseau. Theories of political obligation stand out from other doctrines of the period because of their attempt to justify political authority on grounds of individual self-interest and rational consent. They attempted to demonstrate the value and purposes of organized government by comparing the advantages of civil society with the disadvantages of the state of nature, a hypothetical condition characterized by a complete absence of governmental authority. The purpose of this comparison was to show why and under what conditions government is useful and ought therefore to be accepted by all reasonable people as a voluntary obligation. These conclusions were then reduced to the form of a social contract, from which it was supposed that all the essential rights and duties of citizens could be logically deduced.

Theories of the social contract differed according to their purpose: some were designed to justify the power of the sovereign; conversely, some were intended to safeguard the individual from oppression by an all-too-powerful sovereign.

According to Hobbes (*Leviathan*, 1651), the state of nature was one in which there were no enforceable criteria of right and wrong. Each person took for himself all that he could; human life was "solitary, poor, nasty, brutish and short." The state of nature was therefore a state of war, which could be

(continued on the next page)

ended only if individuals agreed (in a social contract) to give their liberty into the hands of a sovereign, who was thenceforward absolute, on the sole condition that their lives were safeguarded by sovereign power.

Locke (in the second of *Two Treatises of Government*, 1690) differed from Hobbes insofar as he described the state of nature as one in which the rights of life and property were generally recognized under natural law, the inconveniences of the situation arising from insecurity in the enforcement of those rights. He therefore argued that the obligation to obey civil government under the social contract was conditional upon the protection not only of the person but also of private property. If a sovereign violated these terms, he could be justifiably overthrown.

Rousseau (in *Du contrat social*, 1762) held that in the state of nature man was unwarlike and somewhat undeveloped in his reasoning powers and sense of morality and responsibility. When, however, people agreed for mutual protection to surrender individual freedom of action and establish laws and government, they then acquired a sense of moral and civic obligation. In order to retain its essentially moral character, government must thus rest on the consent of the governed, the *volonté générale* ("general will').

The more perceptive social-contract theorists, including Hobbes, invariably recognized that their concepts of the social contract and the state of nature were unhistorical and that they could be justified only as hypotheses useful for the clarification of timeless political problems.

police are needed to secure the individual's life and liberty, but their coercive power may also be turned against him. The problem, then, is to devise a system that gives government the power necessary to protect individual liberty but also prevents those who govern from abusing that power.

The problem is compounded when one asks whether this is all that government can or should do on behalf of individual freedom. Some liberals—the so-called neoclassical liberals, or libertarians—answer that it is. Since the late 19th century, however, most liberals have insisted that the powers of government can promote as well as protect the freedom of the individual. According to modern liberalism, the chief task of government is to remove obstacles that prevent individuals from living freely or from fully realizing their potential. Such obstacles include poverty, disease, discrimination, and ignorance. The disagreement among liberals over whether government should promote individual freedom rather than merely protect it is reflected to some extent in the different prevailing conceptions of liberalism in the United States and Europe since the late 20th century. In the United States liberalism is associated with the welfare-state policies of the New Deal program of the Democratic administration of Pres. Franklin D. Roosevelt, whereas in Europe it is more commonly associated with a commitment to limited government and laissez-faire economic policies.

Liberalism is derived from two related features of Western culture. The first is the West's preoccupation with individuality, as compared to the emphasis in other civilizations on status, caste, and tradition. Throughout much of history, the individual has been submerged in and subordinate to his clan, tribe, ethnic group, or kingdom. Liberalism is the culmination of developments in Western society that produced a sense of the importance of human individuality, a liberation of the individual from complete subservience to the group, and a relaxation of the tight hold of custom, law, and authority. In this respect, liberalism stands for the emancipation of the individual.

Liberalism also derives from the practice of adversariality in European political and economic life, a process in which institutionalized competition—such as the competition between different political parties in electoral contests, between prosecution and defense in adversary procedure, or between different producers in a market economy—generates a dynamic social order. Adversarial systems have always been precarious, however, and it took a long time for the belief in adversariality to emerge from the more traditional view, traceable at least to Plato, that the state should be an organic structure, like a beehive, in which the different social classes cooperate by performing distinct yet complementary roles. The belief that competition is an essential part of a political system and that good government requires a vigorous opposition was still considered strange in most European countries in the early 19th century.

Underlying the liberal belief in adversariality is the conviction that human beings are essentially rational creatures capable of settling their political disputes through dialogue and compromise. This aspect of liberalism became particularly prominent in 20th-century projects aimed at eliminating war and resolving disagreements between states through organizations such as the League of Nations, the United Nations, and the International Court of Justice (World Court).

Liberalism has a close but sometimes uneasy relationship with democracy. At the centre of democratic doctrine is the belief that governments derive their authority from popular election; liberalism, however, is primarily concerned with the scope of governmental activity. Liberals often have been wary of democracy, then, because of fears that it might generate a tyranny by the majority. One might briskly say, therefore, that democracy looks after majorities and liberalism after unpopular minorities.

Like other political doctrines, liberalism is highly sensitive to time and circumstance. Each country's liberalism is different, and it changes in each generation. The historical development of liberalism over recent centuries has been a movement from mistrust of the state's power on the ground that it tends to be misused, to a willingness to use the power of government to correct perceived inequities in the distribution of wealth resulting from economic competition—inequities that purportedly deprive some people of an equal opportunity to live freely. The expansion of governmental power and responsibility sought by liberals in the 20th century was clearly opposed to the contraction of government advocated by liberals a century earlier. In the 19th century liberals generally formed the party of business and the entrepreneurial middle class; for much of the 20th century they were more likely to work to restrict and regulate business in order to provide greater opportunities for labourers and consumers. In each case, however, the liberals' inspiration was the same: a hostility to concentrations of power that threaten the freedom of the individual and prevent him from realizing his full potential, along with a willingness to reexamine and reform social institutions in the light of new needs. This willingness is tempered by an aversion to sudden, cataclysmic change, which is what sets off the liberal from the radical. It is this very eagerness to welcome and encourage useful change, however, that distinguishes the liberal from the conservative, who believes that change is at least as likely to result in loss as in gain.

Distribution of Wealth

Distribution of wealth is the way in which the wealth and income of a nation are divided among its population, or the way in which the wealth and income of the world are divided among nations. Such patterns of distribution are discerned and studied by various statistical means, all of which are based on data of varying degrees of reliability.

Wealth is an accumulated store of possessions and financial claims. It may be given a monetary value if prices can be determined for each of the possessions; this process can be difficult when the possessions are such that they are not likely to be offered for sale. Income is a net total of the flow of payments received in a given time period. Some countries collect statistics on wealth from legally required evaluations of the estates of deceased persons, which may or may not be indicative of what is possessed by the living. In many countries, annual tax statements that measure income provide more or less reliable information. Differences in definitions of income—whether, for example, income should include payments that are transfers rather than the result of productive activity, or capital gains or losses that change the value of an individual's wealth—make comparisons difficult.

To classify patterns of national wealth and income, a basis of classification must be determined. One classification system categorizes wealth and income on the basis of the ownership of factors of production: labour, land, capital, and, occasionally, entrepreneurship, whose respective forms of income are labeled wages, rent, interest, and profit. Personal distribution statistics, usually developed from tax reports, categorize wealth and income on a per capita basis.

Gross national income (GNI) per capita provides a rough measure of annual national income per person in different countries. Countries that have a sizable modern industrial sector have a much higher GNI per capita than countries that are less developed. In the early 21st century, for example, the World Bank estimated that the per-capita GNI was approximately $10,000 and above for the most-developed countries but was less than $825 for the least-developed countries. Income also varies greatly within countries. In a high-income country such as the United States, there is considerable variation among industries, regions, rural and urban areas, females and males, and ethnic groups. While the bulk of the U.S. population has a middle income that is derived largely from earnings, wages vary considerably depending on occupation.

A significant proportion of an economy's higher incomes will derive from investment rather than earnings. It is often the case that the higher the income, the higher the investment-derived portion tends to be. Because most fortunes require long periods to accumulate, the existence of a class of very wealthy persons can result from the ability of those persons to retain their fortunes and pass them on to descendants. Earned incomes are influenced by a different kind of inheritance. Access to well-paid jobs and social status is largely the product of education and opportunity. Typically, therefore, well-educated children of wealthier parents tend to retain their parents' status and earning power. A dynamic economy, however, increases the likelihood of attaining wealth and status through individual effort alone.

Welfare State

A welfare state is a concept of government in which the state plays a key role in the protection and promotion of the economic and social well-being of its citizens. It is based on the principles of equality of opportunity, equitable distribution of wealth, and public responsibility for those unable to avail themselves of the minimal provisions for a good life. The general term may cover a variety of forms of economic and social organization.

A fundamental feature of the welfare state is social insurance, a provision common to most advanced industrialized countries (e.g., National Insurance in the United Kingdom and Social Security in the United States). Such insurance is usually financed by compulsory contributions and is intended to provide benefits to persons and families during periods of greatest need. It is widely recognized, however, that in practice these cash benefits fall considerably short of the levels intended by the designers of the plans.

The welfare state also usually includes public provision of basic education, health services, and housing (in some cases at low cost or without charge). In these respects the welfare state is considerably more extensive in western European countries than in the United States, featuring in many cases comprehensive health coverage and provision of state-subsidized tertiary education.

Antipoverty programs and the system of personal taxation may also be regarded as aspects of the welfare state. Personal taxation falls into this category insofar as its progressivity is used to achieve greater justice in income distribution (rather than merely to raise revenue) and also insofar as it used to finance social insurance payments and other benefits not completely financed by compulsory contributions. In socialist countries the welfare state also covers employment and administration of consumer prices.

The modern use of the term is associated with the comprehensive measures of social insurance adopted in 1948 by Great Britain on the basis of the report on *Social Insurance and Allied Services* (1942) by Sir William (later Lord) Beveridge. In the 20th century, as the earlier concept of the passive laissez-faire state was gradually abandoned, almost all states sought to provide at least some of the measures of social insurance associated with the welfare state. Thus, in the United States the New Deal of Pres. Franklin D. Roosevelt, the Fair Deal of Pres. Harry S. Truman, and a large part of the domestic programs of later presidents were based on welfare state principles. In its more thoroughgoing form, the welfare state provides state aid for the individual in almost all phases of life—"from the cradle to the grave"—as exemplified in the Netherlands and the Social Democratic governments of the Scandinavian countries. Many less-developed countries have the establishment of some form of welfare state as their goal.

The principal problems in the administration of a welfare state are: determining the desirable level of provision of services by the state; ensuring that the system of personal benefits and contributions meets the needs of individuals and families while at the same time offering sufficient incentives for productive work; ensuring efficiency in the operation of state monopolies and bureaucracies; and the equitable provision of resources to finance the services over and above the contributions of direct beneficiaries.

CHAPTER 12

ARISTOTLE'S "IDEAL DEMOCRACY"

Aristotle found it useful to classify actually existing governments in terms of three "ideal constitutions." For essentially the same reasons, the notion of an "ideal democracy" also can be useful for identifying and understanding the democratic characteristics of actually existing governments, be they of city-states, nation-states, or larger associations.

It is important to note that the term *ideal* is ambiguous. In one sense, a system is ideal if it is considered apart from, or in the absence of, certain empirical conditions, which in actuality are always present to some degree. Ideal systems in this sense are used to identify what features of an actual system are essential to it, or what underlying laws are responsible, in combination with empirical factors, for a system's behaviour in

Aristotle proposed that an ideal democracy would incorporate effective participation, equality in voting, an informed electorate, citizen control of the agenda, inclusion, and fundamental rights. thelefty/iStock/ Thinkstock

actual circumstances. In another sense, a system is ideal if it is "best" from a moral point of view. An ideal system in this sense is a goal toward which a person or society ought to strive (even if it is not perfectly attainable in practice) and a standard against which the moral worth of what has been achieved, or of what exists, can be measured.

These two senses are often confused. Systems that are ideal in the first sense may, but need not, be ideal in the second sense. Accordingly, a description of an ideal democracy, such as the one below, need not be intended to prescribe a particular political system. Indeed, influential conceptions of ideal democracy have been offered by democracy's enemies as well as by its friends.

Ideal Democracy's Features

At the very least, an ideal democracy would include the features that follow:

Effective participation. Before a policy is adopted or rejected, members of the *dēmos* have the opportunity to make their views about the policy known to other members.

Equality in voting. Members of the *dēmos* have the opportunity to vote for or against the policy, and all votes are counted as equal.

Informed electorate. Members of the *dēmos* have the opportunity, within a reasonable amount of time, to learn about the policy and about possible alternative policies and their likely consequences.

Citizen control of the agenda. The *dēmos*, and only the *dēmos*, decides what matters are placed on the decision-making agenda and how they are placed there. Thus, the democratic process is "open" in the sense that the *dēmos* can change the policies of the association at any time.

Inclusion. Each and every member of the *dēmos* is entitled to participate in the association in the ways just described.

Fundamental rights. Each of the necessary features of ideal democracy prescribes a right that is itself a necessary feature of ideal democracy: thus every member of the *dēmos* has a right to communicate with others, a right to have his vote counted equally with the votes of others, a right to gather information, a right to participate on an equal footing with other members, and a right, with other members, to exercise control of the agenda. Democracy, therefore, consists of more than just political processes; it is also necessarily a system of fundamental rights.

Ideal Democracy and Representative Democracy

In modern representative democracies, the qualities of ideal democracy, to the degree that they exist, are achieved by way of a myriad of political institutions. These institutions, which are largely analogous in various countries in spite of important differences in constitutional structure, were entirely new in human history at the time of their first appearance in Europe and the United States in the 18th century. Among the most important of them is naturally the institution of representation itself, through which all major government decisions and policies are made by popularly elected officials, who are accountable to the electorate for their actions. Other important institutions include the following:

Free, fair, and frequent elections. Citizens may participate in such elections both as voters and as candidates (though age and residence restrictions may be imposed).

Outside the White House, students exercise their freedom of assembly, protesting that the proposed Keystone XL pipeline through Canada and the Midwestern United States is an environmental hazard. Nicholas Kamm/AFP/Getty Images

Freedom of expression. Citizens may express themselves publicly on a broad range of politically relevant subjects without fear of punishment.

Independent sources of information. There exist sources of political information that are not under the control of the government or any single group and whose right to publish or otherwise disseminate information is protected by law; moreover, all citizens are entitled to seek out and use such sources of information.

Freedom of association. Citizens have the right to form and to participate in independent political organizations, including parties and interest groups.

Institutions like these developed in Europe and the United States in various political and historical circumstances, and the impulses that fostered them were not always themselves democratic. Yet, as they developed, it became increasingly apparent that they were necessary for achieving a satisfactory level of democracy in any political association as large as a nation-state.

The relation between these institutions and the features of ideal democracy that are realized through them can be summarized as follows. In an association as large as a nation-state, representation is necessary for effective participation and for citizen control of the agenda; free, fair, and frequent elections are necessary for effective participation and for equality in voting; and freedom of expression, independent sources of information, and freedom of association are each necessary for effective participation, an informed electorate, and citizen control of the agenda.

The Four Freedoms

The Four Freedoms were a formulation of worldwide social and political objectives by U.S. Pres. Franklin D. Roosevelt in the State of the Union message he delivered to Congress on Jan. 6, 1941. Roosevelt stated these freedoms to be the freedom of speech and expression, the freedom of every person to worship God in his own way, the freedom from want, and the freedom from fear. Roosevelt called for ensuring the latter through "a world-wide reduction of armaments to such a point and in such a thorough fashion that no nation will be in a position to commit an act of physical aggression against any neighbor—anywhere in the world."

Approaching Actual Democracy

In general, political philosophers since the days of Aristotle tend to firmly believe that it is unlikely any actual political system can fully achieve all the characteristics of its equivalent ideal. Thus, whereas the institutions of many actual systems are sufficient to attain a relatively high level of democracy, they are almost certainly not sufficient to achieve anything like perfect or ideal democracy. Nevertheless, such institutions may produce a satisfactory approximation of the ideal—as presumably they did in Athens in the 5th century BCE, when the term *democracy* was coined, and in the United States in the early 19th century, when Tocqueville, like most others in America and elsewhere, unhesitatingly called the country a democracy.

For associations that are small in population and area, the political institutions of direct democracy seem best to approximate the ideal of "government by the people." In such a democracy all matters of importance to the association as a whole can be decided on by the citizens. Citizens have the opportunity to discuss the policies that come before them and to gather information directly from those they consider well-informed, as well as from other sources. They can meet at a convenient place—the Pnyx in Athens, the Forum in Rome, the Palazzo Ducale in Venice, or the town hall in a New England village—to discuss the policy further and to offer amendments or revisions. Finally, their decision is rendered in a vote, all votes being counted equal, with the votes of a majority prevailing.

It is thus easy to see why direct democracies are sometimes thought to approach ideal democracy much more closely than representative systems ever could and why the most ardent advocates of direct democracy have sometimes insisted, as Rousseau did in *The Social Contract*, that the term *representative democracy* is self-contradictory. Yet, views like these have failed to win many converts.

The Value of Democracy

On what grounds is it decided that "the people" should rule or whether democracy is truly better than other forms of government? Although a full exploration of this issue is beyond the scope of this chapter, history—particularly 20th-century history—demonstrates that democracy uniquely possesses a number of features that most people, whatever their basic political beliefs, would consider desirable: (1) democracy helps to prevent rule by cruel and vicious autocrats; (2) modern representative democracies do not fight wars with one another; (3) countries with democratic governments tend to be more prosperous than countries with nondemocratic governments; and (4) democracy tends to foster human development—as measured by health, education, personal income, and other indicators—more fully than other forms of government do. Other features of democracy also would be considered desirable by most people, though some would regard them as less important than (1) through (4) above: (5) democracy helps people to protect their fundamental interests; (6) democracy guarantees its citizens fundamental rights that nondemocratic systems do not, and cannot, grant; and (7) democracy ensures its citizens a broader range of personal freedoms than other forms of government do. Finally, there are some features of democracy that some people—the critics of democracy—would not consider desirable at all, though most people, upon reflection, would regard them as at least worthwhile: (8) only democracy provides people with a maximum opportunity to live under laws of their own choosing; (9) only democracy provides people with a maximum opportunity to take moral responsibility for their choices and decisions about government policies; and (10) only in a democracy can there be a relatively high level of political equality.

These advantages notwithstanding, there have been critics of democracy since ancient times. Perhaps the most enduring of their charges is that most people are incapable of participating in government in a meaningful or competent way because they lack the necessary knowledge, intelligence, wisdom, experience, or character. According to Plato, for example, the best government would be an aristocracy of "philosopher-kings" whose rigorous intellectual and moral training would make them uniquely qualified to rule. The view that the people as a whole are incapable of governing themselves has been espoused not only by kings and aristocratic rulers but also by political theorists (Plato foremost among them), religious leaders, and other authorities. The view was prevalent in one form or another throughout the world during most of recorded history until the early 20th century, and since then it has been most often invoked by opponents of democracy in Europe and elsewhere to justify various forms of dictatorship and one-party rule.

No doubt there will be critics of democracy for as long as democratic governments exist. The extent of their success in winning adherents and promoting the creation of nondemocratic regimes will depend on how well democratic governments meet the new challenges and crises that are all but certain to occur.

CHAPTER 13

DEMOCRACY'S PROBLEMS AND CHALLENGES

At the onset of the 21st century, democracy was confronted with many challenges, both old and new.

Disparity of Resources

Decentralized market economies stimulated democracy's expansion, but in countries where they were inadequately controlled such economies ultimately created vast disparities in economic and social supplies, from wealth and income to education and social status. Because those with greater resources naturally tended to use them to influence the political system to their advantage, the existence of such inequalities constituted a persistent obstacle to the achievement of a satisfactory level of political equality. This challenge was magnified during regularly occurring economic downturns, when poverty and unemployment tended to increase.

Immigrants

Following the Second World War, immigration to western Europe, Australia, and the United States—legal as well as illegal—soared. Fleeing poverty or oppression in their homelands the often uneducated immigrants primarily from the developing world typically took menial

Immigrants, such as these Mexican migrant workers picking spinach in Colorado, often work in agriculture because they struggle to find more skilled jobs. John Moore/Getty Images

jobs in service industries or agriculture. Differences in language, culture, and appearance between immigrant groups and the citizens of the host country, as well as the usually widespread perception that immigrants take jobs away from citizens and use expensive social services, made immigration a hotly debated issue in many countries. In some instances, anti-immigrant sentiment contributed to the rise of radical political parties and movements, such as the National Front in France, the Republicans in Germany, the militia movement in the United States, and the skinhead movement in the United States and Britain. Some of these groups promoted racist or neofascist doctrines that were hostile not only to immigrants but also to fundamental political and human rights and even to democracy itself.

Acts of Terrorism

Terrorism is generally defined as the systematic use of violence to create a general climate of fear in a population and thereby to bring about a particular political objective. Terrorism has been practiced by political organizations with both rightist and leftist objectives, by nationalistic and religious groups, by revolutionaries, and even by state institutions such as armies, intelligence services, and police.

Acts of terrorism committed within democratic countries or against their interests in other parts of the world occurred with increasing frequency beginning in the 1970s. In the United States remarkably few terrorist attacks had taken place before the 1993 bombing of the World Trade Center in New York City. The deadliest single act of terrorism anywhere,

On September 11, 2001, al-Qaeda terrorists flew planes into both towers of the World Trade Center. The attacks led to tighter security measures, which some people criticized for infringing upon civil liberties. Carmen Taylor/ WireImage/Getty Images

the September 11 attacks of 2001, destroyed the World Trade Center and killed some 3,000 people, mainly in New York City and Washington, D.C.

In response to such events, and especially in the wake of the September 11 attacks, democratic governments adopted various measures designed to enhance the ability of police and other law-enforcement agencies to protect their countries against terrorism. Some of these initiatives entailed new restrictions on citizens' civil and political liberties and were accordingly criticized as unconstitutional or otherwise inconsistent with democratic principles. In the early 21st century it remained to be seen whether democratic governments could strike a satisfactory balance between the sometimes conflicting imperatives of ensuring security and preserving democracy.

September 11th

Nineteen militants connected to al-Qaeda, an Islamic extremist group, perpetrated a string of airline hijackings and suicide attacks against U.S. targets, known as the September 11 attacks or 9/11 attacks. They were the deadliest terrorist attacks on American soil in U.S. history. The attacks against New York City and Washington, D.C., caused extensive death and destruction and triggered an enormous U.S. effort to combat terrorism. Some 2,750 people were killed in New York, 184 at the Pentagon, and 40 in Pennsylvania (where one of the hijacked planes crashed after the passengers attempted to retake the plane); all 19 terrorists died. Police and fire departments in New York were especially hard-hit: hundreds had rushed to the scene of the attacks, and more than 400 police officers and firefighters were killed.

Terrorism appears to be an enduring feature of political life. Even prior to the September 11 attacks, there was widespread

(continued on the next page)

concern that terrorists might escalate their destructive power to vastly greater proportions by using weapons of mass destruction—including nuclear, biological, or chemical weapons—as was done by the Japanese doomsday cult AUM Shinrikyo, which released nerve gas into a Tokyo subway in 1995. These fears were intensified after September 11, when a number of letters contaminated with anthrax were delivered to political leaders and journalists in the United States, leading to several deaths. U.S. Pres. George W. Bush made a broad war against terrorism the centrepiece of U.S. foreign policy at the beginning of the 21st century.

International Systems

As the 18th century drew to a close, in reaction to the size predicament described previously, the theory as well as the practice of democracy began to focus on the large nation-state instead of the far smaller association of the city-state. Although their increased size enabled democracies to solve more of the problems they confronted, there remained some problems that not even the largest democracy could solve by itself. To address these problems several international organizations were established after World War II, most notably the United Nations (1945), and their numbers and responsibilities grew rapidly through the rest of the 20th century.

These organizations posed two related challenges to democracy. First, by shifting ultimate control of a country's policies in a certain area to the international level, they reduced to a corresponding extent the influence that citizens could exert on such policies through democratic means. Second, all international organizations, even those that were formally accountable to national governments, lacked the political institutions of representative democracy.

How could these institutions be made democratic—or at least more democratic?

In their struggle to forge a constitution for the new European Union at the beginning of the 21st century, European leaders faced both of these challenges, as well as most of the fundamental questions posed at the beginning of this article. What kind of association is appropriate to a democratic government of Europe? What persons or entities should constitute the European *dēmos*? What political organizations or institutions are needed? Should decisions be made by majority? If so, by what kind of majority—a majority of persons, of countries, of both countries and persons, or of something else? Do all the conditions necessary for satisfactory democratic government exist in this huge and diverse association? If not, would a less democratic system be more desirable?

Transition, Consolidation, Breakdown

For many of the countries that made a transition to democracy in the late 20th and early 21st centuries, the problems and challenges facing democracy were particularly acute. Obstacles in the path of a successful consolidation of democratic institutions included economic problems such as widespread poverty, unemployment, massive inequalities in income and wealth, rapid inflation, and low or negative rates of economic growth. Countries at low levels of economic development also usually lacked a large middle class and a well-educated population. In many of these countries, the division of the population into antagonistic ethnic, racial, religious, or linguistic groups made it difficult to manage political differences peacefully. In others,

Aung San Suu Kyi

Aung San Suu Kyi is the leader of the opposition to the ruling military government in Myanmar (formerly Burma). Aung San Suu Kyi brought international attention to the struggle for human rights and the restoration of democracy in her country. An advocate of nonviolent protest, she was under house arrest in Yangon when she was awarded the 1991 Nobel Prize for Peace.

Aung San Suu Kyi was born on June 19, 1945, in Rangoon (now Yangon). Her father, Aung San, was regarded as the founder of modern Burma after he negotiated the country's independence from Britain. He was assassinated in 1947. Her mother, Khin Kyi, a prominent diplomat, was named ambassador to India in 1960. After studying in India, Aung San Suu Kyi earned a bachelor's degree at the University of Oxford, where she met her future husband, British scholar Michael Aris. She subsequently worked for the United Nations in New York City and in 1985–86 was a visiting scholar in Southeast Asian studies at Kyoto University in Japan. She returned to Burma in April 1988 to care for her ailing mother, who died later that year.

By the end of 1988 Suu Kyi was heavily involved in the protest movements sweeping the country against the brutal rule of military strongman Ne Win. She initiated a nonviolent struggle for democracy and human rights, helping to form the National League for Democracy (NLD), a political party. In July 1989 the military government of newly named Myanmar placed her under house arrest. The military offered to free her if she agreed to leave Myanmar, but she refused to do so until the country was returned to civilian government. In the 1990 parliamentary elections, the NLD won more than 80 percent of the seats that were contested. The military government ignored the election results, however, and did not allow the new parliament to meet. *Freedom from Fear: And Other Writings*, a collection of her articles and speeches edited by Aris, was published in 1991 following the Nobel Prize announcement. Suu Kyi was eventually freed from house arrest in July 1995.

Despite her release, Suu Kyi was officially barred from leading the NLD, and her movements remained restricted. In 1998 she announced the formation of a representative committee that she declared was the country's legitimate ruling parliament. The military regime once again placed her under house arrest from September 2000 to May 2002.

Following clashes between the NLD and pro-government demonstrators in 2003, the government returned Suu Kyi to house arrest. The international community continued to call for her release. In May 2009, shortly before her sentence was to be completed, an intruder (a U.S. citizen) entered her house compound and spent two nights there. Suu Kyi was arrested and convicted of breaching the terms of her house arrest.

It was widely believed that this conviction was intended to prevent her from participating in the 2010 multiparty parliamentary elections—the first to be held since 1990. Indeed, in 2010 new election laws barred individuals who had been convicted of a crime from participating. They also prohibited anyone who was married to a foreign national (as she was) from running for office. In support of Suu Kyi, the NLD refused to reregister under these new laws (as was required) and was disbanded. In the November 2010 elections, the government parties won an overwhelming majority of legislative seats amid widespread allegations of voter fraud. Six days after the elections, Suu Kyi was released from house arrest. She vowed to continue her opposition to military rule.

Government restrictions on Suu Kyi's activities were further relaxed during 2011. She was allowed to meet with Myanmar's new civilian president as well as the prime minister of Thailand and the U.S. secretary of state. Meanwhile, rules on political participation were eased, and the NLD was officially reinstated. Suu Kyi was permitted to run for parliament in elections in April 2012. She easily won a seat representing Yangon. Later in 2012 she traveled outside Myanmar for the first time since 1988. On a tour of Europe, Suu Kyi gave the acceptance speech for her 1991 Nobel Prize in Oslo, Norway, and she addressed the British Parliament in London, England.

extensive government intervention in the economy, along with other factors, resulted in the widespread corruption of government officials. Many countries also lacked an effective legal system, making civil rights highly insecure and allowing for abuse by political elites and criminal elements. In these countries the idea of the rule of law was not well established in the prevailing political culture, in some cases because of constant warfare or long years of authoritarian rule. In other respects the political culture of these countries did not inculcate in citizens the kinds of beliefs and values that could support democratic institutions and practices during crises or even during the ordinary conflicts of political life.

In light of these circumstances, it is quite possible that the extraordinary pace of democratization begun in the 20th century will not continue long into the 21st century. In some countries, authoritarian systems probably will remain in place. In some countries that have made the transition to democracy, new democratic institutions probably will remain weak and fragile. Other countries might lose their democratic governments and revert to some form of authoritarian rule.

Yet, despite these adversities, the odds are great that in the foreseeable future a very large share of the world's population, in a very large share of the world's countries, will live under democratic forms of government that continue to evolve in order to meet challenges both old and new.

CONCLUSION

Democracy is a complex concept that emerged from classical political thought and has since evolved through a number of incarnations, all emphasizing the preservation of individuals' liberty and equality and governance by a rule of law. While hallmarks of a well-functioning democracy include the protection of citizens' rights and liberties and their ability to participate equally in the political process, a number of factors in recent decades raise important complexities as to the true—and proper—reach of democratic principles being carried into action.

Rising economic inequality in many parts of the world—and quite notably in the United States—has important implications with respect to political participation and in turn, the interests that are represented in federal and perhaps even local government. The growth of corporations has given rise to new debates over the proper extent of campaign finance regulation and thus the extent to which governments balance speech through campaign contributions and leveling the playing field in political representation. The introduction of new technologies likewise fundamentally reshapes democratic practices and the reach of equality of representation, with a number of recent legal debates over such matters as privacy and speech—particularly in time of war—but also the dispensing of political information vital to an informed citizenry. The remainder of the 21st century thus provides a number of new opportunities to consider the roots of modern democratic government and contemporary fidelity to its core principles amid a changing economic and technological environment.

GLOSSARY

Bill of Rights A summary of fundamental rights and privileges guaranteed to a people against violation by the state—used especially of the first 10 amendments to the United States Constitution.

capitalism An economic system characterized by private ownership of the means of production, in which prices, production, and the distribution of goods and income are determined mainly by competition in a free market.

compulsory voting A system in which electors are obliged to vote in elections or attend a polling place on the election day.

coup d'état A sudden overthrowing of a government by a small group.

democracy A government in which the supreme power is vested in the people and exercised by them directly or indirectly through a system of representation usually involving periodically held free elections.

despotism A system of government in which the ruler has unlimited power.

direct democracy A form of government in which the entire body of qualified citizens directly makes political decisions.

electoral college A constitutionally mandated process for electing the president and vice president of the United States. Each state appoints as many electors as it has senators and representatives in Congress. A candidate must win 270 of the 538 votes to win the election.

European Union An economic and political union of 28 member states that are located primarily in Europe and operating through intergovernmental negotiated decisions by member states.

faction A party or group (as within a government) that is often contentious or self-seeking.

federalism A political system that binds a group of states into a larger, noncentralized, superior state while allowing them to maintain their own political identities.

gerrymander To divide (a territorial unit) into election districts to give one political party an electoral majority in a large number of districts while concentrating the voting strength of the opposition in as few districts as possible.

gross national income (GNI) A rough measure of annual national income per person in different countries.

initiative A procedure enabling a specified number of voters by petition to propose a law and secure its submission to the electorate or to the legislature for approval.

judiciary The branch of government in which judicial power is vested. The principal work of any judiciary is the adjudication of disputes or controversies.

liberalism Political doctrine that takes protecting and enhancing the freedom of the individual to be the central problem of politics.

lictors Ancient Roman officers who bore the fasces as the insignia of their office and whose duties included accompanying the chief magistrates in public appearances.

majoritarian One who believes in majoritarianism, or a philosophy or practice according to which decisions of the organized group should be made by a numerical majority of its members.

malapportionment Characterized by an inequitable or unsuitable apportioning of representatives to a legislative body; that is, the creation of electoral districts with divergent ratios of voters to representatives.

monarchy Undivided rule or absolute sovereignty by a single person.

oligarchy A government in which a small group exercises control, especially for corrupt and selfish purposes.

parliamentary system A system of government having the real executive power vested in a cabinet composed of members of the legislature who are individually and collectively responsible to the legislature.

presidential system A system of government in which a head of government is also the head of state and leads an executive branch that is constitutionally independent of the legislature.

primary election In the United States, an election to select candidates to run for public office.

proportional representation A system in which representation of parties in a legislature is in proportion to their share of the popular vote.

recall A method of election in which voters can oust an elected official before his or her official term has ended.

referendum The principle or practice of submitting to popular vote a measure passed on or proposed by a legislative body or by popular initiative.

representative democracy A government in which the many are represented by persons chosen from among them usually by election.

republic A government in which supreme power resides in a body of citizens entitled to vote and is exercised by elected officers and representatives responsible to them and governing according to law.

semipresidential system A system of government in which a directly elected president with some executive powers and a premier appointed by the president must retain majority support in the legislature.

social contract An actual or hypothetical agreement among the members of an organized society or between a community and its ruler that defines and limits the rights and duties of each.

suffrage The right to vote.

Tory Party A conservative British party in the 17th through 19th centuries that operated in opposition to the Whig Party.

unilineal Tracing descent through either the maternal or paternal line only.

unitary system A system of political organization in which most or all of the governing power resides in a centralized government and which contrasts with a federal system.

utilitarianism A doctrine that the useful is the good and that the determining consideration of right conduct should be the usefulness of its consequences.

welfare state A concept of government in which the state plays a key role in the protection and promotion of the economic and social well-being of its citizens, based on the principles of equality of opportunity, equitable distribution of wealth, and public responsibility for those unable to avail themselves of the minimal provisions for a good life.

Whig Party A major British political group of the late 17th through early 19th centuries that sought to limit the royal authority and increase parliamentary power.

BIBLIOGRAPHY

Classic Texts

Classic treatments of democracy and other forms of government are widely available in numerous editions. They include Plato, *The Republic;* Aristotle, *Politics;* Niccolò Machiavelli, *The Prince* (1513), and *Discourses on the First Ten Books of Livy* (1513); Thomas Hobbes, *Leviathan, or the Matter, Form, and Power of a Commonwealth, Ecclesiastical and Civil* (1651); John Locke, *Second Treatise of Civil Government* (1690); Montesquieu, *The Spirit of the Laws* (1748); Jean-Jacques Rousseau, *The Social Contract* (1762); Alexander Hamilton, James Madison, and John Jay, *The Federalist* (1788), containing 77 of the 85 Federalist papers; Thomas Paine, *Rights of Man* (1791); Alexis de Tocqueville, *Democracy in America*, 4 vol. (1835–40); John Stuart Mill, *On Liberty* (1859), and *Considerations on Representative Government* (1861); John Dewey, *The Public and Its Problems* (1927, reissued 1991); Jürgen Habermas, *The Theory of Communicative Action*, trans. from the German by Thomas McCarthy, 2 vol. (1984, reissued 1987); and John Rawls, *A Theory of Justice* (1971), and *Political Liberalism* (1993).

Noteworthy discussions in the secondary literature include John Dunn, *The Political Thought of John Locke* (1966, reissued 1975); Richard Fralin, *Rousseau and Representation* (1978); Robert B. Westbrook, *John Dewey and American Democracy* (1991); and Thomas McCarthy, *The Critical Theory of Jürgen Habermas* (1978, reissued 1984).

Democratic Institutions

A concise introduction is Alan F. Hattersley, *A Short History of Democracy* (1930). Historical and theoretical approaches are combined in John Dunn (ed.), *Democracy: The Unfinished Journey, 508 BC to AD 1993* (1992, reprinted with corrections 1993); and Sanford Lakoff, *Democracy: History, Theory, and Practice* (1996).

General works on ancient Greece include I.E.S. Edwards et al. (eds.), *The Cambridge Ancient History*, 3rd ed., 14 vol. (1970–2000); and Thomas R. Martin, *Ancient Greece: From Prehistoric Times to Hellenistic Times*, updated ed. (2000). A.H.M. Jones, *Athenian Democracy* (1957, reissued 1986), is indispensable, particularly as a corrective to Plato, Aristotle, and Thucydides. The most comprehensive study of democracy in Athens is Mogens Herman Hansen, *The Athenian Democracy in the Age of Demosthenes*, trans. from the Danish by J.A. Crook (1991, reissued 1999).

A brief account of Rome's republican government is F.E. Adcock, *Roman Political Ideas and Practice* (1959, reissued 1972). An excellent, though critical, account of the Italian city-state republics is Lauro Martines, *Power and Imagination: City-States in Renaissance Italy* (1979, reissued 2002). Also of interest are J.K. Hyde, *Society and Politics in Medieval Italy* (1973); and Quentin Skinner, "The Italian City-State Republics," in Dunn (ed.), *Democracy: The Unfinished Journey, 508 BC to AD 1993* (1992, reprinted with corrections 1993).

An essential source on the development of cabinet government in Britain is Archibald S. Foord, *His Majesty's Opposition, 1714–1830* (1964, reissued 1979). The classic 1867 work by Walter Bagehot, *The English Constitution*, ed. by Miles Taylor (2001), remains highly informative.

The Theory of Democracy

The theory, foundations, and institutions of democracy are described in Giovanni Sartori, *Democratic Theory* (1961, reissued 1973); C.B. Macpherson, *Democratic Theory: Essays in Retrieval*

(1973); Robert A. Dahl, *Democracy and Its Critics* (1989, reissued 1991), and *On Democracy* (1998, reissued 2001); and Ian Shapiro, *Democracy's Place* (1996).

Elections

A classic English-language review of the history of elections is Charles Seymour and Donald Paige Frary, *How the World Votes: The Story of Democratic Development in Elections*, 2 vol. (1918). A readable, comprehensive overview of electoral institutions is David M. Farrell, *Electoral Systems: A Comparative Introduction* (2001). The impact of electoral systems on party systems is analyzed in Douglas W. Rae, *The Political Consequences of Electoral Laws*, rev. ed. (1971); Rein Taagepera and Matthew Soberg Shugart, *Seats and Votes: The Effects and Determinants of Electoral Systems* (1989, reissued 1991); and Arend Lijphart et al., *Electoral Systems and Party Systems: A Study of Twenty-seven Democracies, 1945–1990* (1994). The significance for democratic theory of electoral arrangements is considered in Richard S. Katz, *Democracy and Elections* (1997). The development of mixed-member electoral systems is the focus of Matthew Soberg Shugart and Martin P. Wattenberg (eds.), *Mixed-Member Electoral Systems: The Best of Both Worlds?* (2001).

Analyses of referenda and direct democracy can be found in David B. Magleby, *Direct Legislation: Voting on Ballot Propositions in the United States* (1984); Thomas E. Cronin, *Direct Democracy: The Politics of Initiative, Referendum, and Recall* (1989, reissued 1999); David Butler and Austin Ranney (eds.), *Referendums Around the World: The Growing Use of Direct Democracy* (1994); and Ian Budge, *The New Challenge of Direct Democracy* (1996).

Classic perspectives on voting behaviour and electoral participation can be found in Anthony Downs, *An Economic Theory of Democracy* (1957, reissued 1965); Angus Campbell et al., *The American Voter* (1960, reprinted 1980); and Seymour M. Lipset and Stein Rokkan (eds.), *Party Systems and Voter Alignments: Cross-National Perspectives* (1967). Other developments in voting behaviour are discussed in Ivor Crewe and David Denver (eds.), *Electoral Change in Western Democracies: Patterns and Sources of Electoral Volatility* (1985); Stefano Bartolini and Peter Mair, *Identity, Competition and Electoral Availability: The Stabilisation of European Electorates, 1885–1985* (1990); Mark N. Franklin et al., *Electoral Change: Responses to Evolving Social and Attitudinal Structures in Western Countries* (1992); Samuel L. Popkin, *The Reasoning Voter: Communication and Persuasion in Presidential Campaigns*, 2nd ed. (1994); Warren E. Miller and J. Merrill Shanks, *The New American Voter* (1996); Geoffrey Evans (ed.), *The End of Class Politics?: Class Voting in Comparative Context* (1999); and Samuel Merrill III and Bernard Grofman, *A Unified Theory of Voting: Directional and Proximity Spatial Models* (1999).

Problems and Challenges

Contemporary problems and challenges are discussed in Ian Shapiro and Casiano Hacker-Cordón (eds.), *Democracy's Edges* (1999); Keith Dowding, James Hughes, and Helen Margetts (eds.), *Challenges to Democracy* (2001); and Sergio Fabbrini (ed.), *Nation, Federalism and Democracy* (2001). Some implications of democratic ideas for nongovernmental organizations are examined in Robert A. Dahl, *A Preface to Economic Democracy* (1985); and Ian Shapiro, *Democratic Justice* (1999, reissued 2001).

INDEX

A

additional-member system, 107–108
Althing, Icelandic, 51, 52, 98
American Civil War, 72, 87, 96, 125
American Revolution, 23, 55, 58, 60, 61
Andrae, Carl, 105
Anne, Queen, 54
Anthony, Susan B., 87
Apollodorus of Damascus, 25, 26
aristocracy, 3, 4, 8, 10, 17, 23, 44, 50, 75, 97, 111, 160, 185
Aristotle, 17–18, 38, 44, 167
    "ideal democracy" of, 180–187
Articles of Confederation, 58, 61–63, 66, 78
Athens, ancient, 1, 5, 9, 11, 12–13, 15, 16, 18, 21, 22, 110, 185
Augustus, 26, 29, 33
Aung San Suu Kyi, 194–195
authoritarianism, 113, 196

B

balloting, 150–152
Beaumont, Gustave de, 76
Bill of Rights, 62, 64, 71–72, 93–96, 103
Bodin, Jean, 23
Bundestag, German, 139
Burr, Aaron, 125

C

Caesar, Julius, 26, 29, 33
censor, 30–31
Cephalus, 13
checks and balances, 66, 79, 90, 98
civil liberties, 71–72
Civil Rights Act (1964), 83–85
Cleisthenes of Athens, 9, 12, 15, 18–20
Comitia Centuriata, 22, 27, 30–31
Comitia Curiata, 22, 31
Comitia Tributa, 22
communism, 107, 112, 161
compulsory voting, 152–154
Concilium Plebis, 22
Congress, U.S., 64, 66, 67, 68–69, 70, 88, 94, 95, 128
Considerations on Representative Government, 49, 81
Constantine I, 29, 34
constituencies, districting and apportionment, 142–147
Constitution, U.S., 42, 58, 61, 62, 63–73, 74, 76, 78–79, 87, 88, 89, 97, 103, 123, 124
    Bill of Rights, 62, 64, 71–72, 93–96
    civil liberties and the Bill of Rights, 71–72
    Constitutional Convention, 59, 62, 63–66, 74, 75, 89, 92